HOW TO DOUBLE THE MEANING OF LIFE

by Anil

with drawings by

Jasmine Jordan

ONE OUT OF TEN PEOPLE RECOMMENDS THIS BOOK

Library of Congress Control Number: 2011907840

ISBN:	Hardcover	978-1-4628-7121-6
	Softcover	978-1-4628-7120-9
	Ebook	978-1-4568-9384-2

To order additional copies of this book, contact:

Xlibris Corporation

1-800-618-969

www.xlibris.com.au

Orders@xlibris.com.au

500669

HOW TO DOUBLE

THE MEANING OF LIFE

IN FIVE ACTS

Anil

drawings by Jasmine Jordan

The marvellous thing about a joke with a double meaning is that it can only mean one thing. — *Ronnie Barker*

Talking nonsense is man's only privilege that distinguishes him from all other organisms. — *Fyodor Dostoyevsky*

Act I. PUN FUN (cornycopia, confusions say)

Act II. PANDORA'S DICTIONARY (coinages, satire)

Act III. SOUNDS ALIKE FUN (ear puns, rhymes)

Act IV. LETTER RIP (anagrams, palindromes, etc)

Act V. PROSE AND CONS (one-liners, jokes)

THANKS

My personal editor Sue Melton (suzemelton@verizon.net) has contributed very significantly to this "five-act play" on words, primarily by helping me to admit to and eliminate mountains of inferior puns and other critters. You too should thank her for that! But both she and Jasmine disavow any knowledge of me or my whereabouts when I get too rude, gross or opinionated, including a few of the drawings I had to force Jasmine to draw at gunpoint.

I also thank those who encouraged me over the years and inspired me to carry on with this nonsense. Notably, A. Ross Eckler and Jeremiah Farrell (past and present editors of *Word Ways*), Martin Gardner, David Morice, Howard Bergerson, Peter Jeffery, Anne Graham, Robert McGough, Graeme Bell, John O'Brien, John Hall-Freeman, Marilynn Goldsmith and Marcia Landy, plus many others, including my favourite humorists, too numerous to name, but especially Walt Kelly, James Thurber, Mark Twain, Spike Milligan, Monty Python, Lily Tomlin, Robin Williams, Douglas Adams, Ray Waterson, Gary Larson, Michael Leunig, all of whom contributed by influencing the warp of my humour.

Some of the material in all acts, especially IV, is from *Word Ways: the Journal of Recreational Linguistics*, 2001-2010; wordways@butler.edu. Interjections attributed to *Ed.* are fictitious, usually but not always obvious. I use quite a lot of quotations throughout as leavening and pepper, hoping thereby to gain favour by association. They are indexed by author at the end of act V. A majority are found in these excellent collections:

Dim Wit, ed. Rosemarie Jarski, Ebury Press, 2008

Funny You Should Say That, ed. Andrew Martin, Penguin, 2005

The Penguin Dictionary of Modern Humorous Quotations, ed. Fred Metcalf, 2001

Cassell Dictionary of Humorous Quotations, ed. Nigel Rees, 1998

Cassell Dictionary of Insulting Quotations, ed. Jonathon Green, 1996

(John S.) *Crosbie's Dictionary of Puns*, NY: Harmony, 1977

The ability to quote is a serviceable substitute for wit.

— *W. Somerset Maugham*

OVERALL INTRODUCTION

Is the meaning of life to find the meaning of life? I dunno, I'm just meeting my contractual obligation to double "the meaning of life" and maximise groans as I offer up a f(e)ast of twisted word play, a pundemonium of fun, nonsense and satire. This isn't the sequel to Monty Python's *The Meaning of Life*, by the way, nor a claim to be twice as funny. Not by half! It's the ~~work~~ play of a **psycho linguist** who *loves words to death*, a **wordo word phonetic** who engages our disgustingly ambiguous language in battle, daring a term to have but one reading, mocking and killing any I can find a joke in, bisecting them with blows from my **wordswords** into a dead, useless term and a live, useless pun.

If you don't believe life has a meaning worth doubling, I offer ***How to Double the Meaninglessness of Life*:**

I can't think of anything worse after a night of drinking than waking up next to someone and not being able to remember their name or how you met or why they're dead.
— Laura Kightlinger

The very notion of playing with words is an assault on propriety, adding to the glee of course. Words are one of three things my mother told me not to play with. (Another was my food.) "Son, don't play with your words!" That exclamation remark rings on in my tortured conscience as I disobey her in extremis.

The five acts of this play represent different styles of wordplay. Acts I-1V, each with a special twist or formula, are mostly organised dictionary style within each chapter. Act V is more prosaic. I is pure silliness but II-V mix in some satire. I call individual items critters to affect a down home ambience while maintaining an artistic conceit. Let me know if you're fooled, y'hear?

Except for a few oldies with a new twist, I've tried to use only original puns, but that may be the biggest joke of all. The same puns occur to many people over the years, unrecorded. Even knowing all the "public" puns is impossible as they are tucked away in an untold myriad of sources, or presented but not recorded.

Act I.

Punning or paronomasia is an activity almost everyone has engaged in at some high point in their lives. Punning thrives on ambiguity if not being its synonym, both meaning two or more meanings.

This Act specialises in plain old corn. If you're not a vegetarian and prefer a meatier dose, skip to any of the other four acts in the play. But if you just want a giggle, an aha, a moan or an occasional guffaw, sit tight.

Chapter 1. **CORNYCOPIA**

Here be a FICTIONARY or dictionary of misdefinitions, aka "daffynitions", a format also used in most other chapters in acts I, II, and half of III and IV.

"Punning is the lowest form of wit!" It is so, and therefore the foundation of all wit.
— *Anon.*

A pun is the lowest form of humour—when you don't think of it first.
— *Oscar Levant*

The pun is the lowest form of humus—earthy wit that everyone digs.
— *John Crosbie*

There are three rules to comedy: 1. No puns. 2. No puns. 3. No puns.
— *John Cleese* (4. No shit?)

I never knew an enemy to puns who was not an ill-natured man.
— *Charles Lamb* (Cleese?)

A pun is a pistol let off at the ear; not a feather to tickle the intellect.
— *Charles Lamb* (Ill-natured?)

Of puns it has been said that those who most dislike them are those who are least able to utter them.
— *Edgar Allan Poe* (Yay! A fight between Poe and Cleese!!)

It seems that no one enjoys any puns except his own.
— *Louis Untermeyer* *(Ouch! I hope not.)*

On occasion, a pun can seem humorous to others, too.
— *David Morice* (That's my hope, Dave. Thanks!)

Science has not found a cure for the pun.
— *Robt. Byrne* (What a relief. *But they will!)*

Killing a punster could be justified if the pun is bad enough.
— *Oliver Wendell Holmes*

But recall this VIP very important pun in US history:

We must all hang together or assuredly we shall all hang separately.
— *Benjamin Franklin*

absentminded wishing to be elsewhere

airtight too many in-flight drinks *(airtight but not leakproof)*

all out effort a poor inning for the batting side

anal retentive what the toilet paper missed
anus the benefactory muscle
As in, Give a shit! Don't be an anal retentive tightass! Let go of it! Give back!

Anonymous Anonymous
a help group for profile
challenged people who
don't want it known
that they're unknown
(They meet secretly and
will resent this exposé.)

arctic hare Brrr Rabbit

Assembly of God
a do-it-yourself Deity kit

basket case a container container
cancan ditto (Even a **vacant** container container is still a **can** in a **vat**.)

The other day I bought a wastepaper basket and carried it home in a paper bag. And when I got home, I put the bag in the basket. — *Lily Tomlin*

barefoot a lucky charm worn by giant aliens for good luck

bartender Dan'l Boone and Davy Crockett's favorite dish
Giant aliens also like bartenders.

bad egg **egg roll**

Mother Nature agrees. Animals rarely have cubical eggs.

Cubical eggs would solve this problem. If Mother Nature is so smart why didn't she think of this?

big dipper

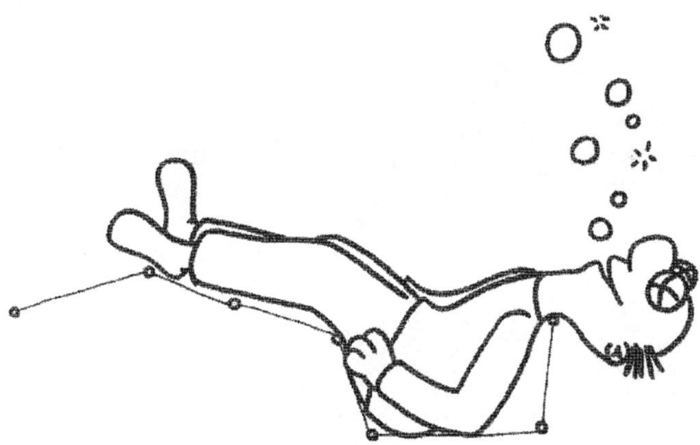

Big Foot a leg-end

birth certificate how to prove you were born
birthday suit how to challenge this in court

bisexual what you ride after outgrowing your trisexual
...ending a ménage à trike.

body building the morgue

bottom drawer artist with a buttocks fixation (or a card cheat)

bringing up a child

Is this what they mean by biofeedback?

bully for you a gift to a masochist

burial grounds Must be dead.

butt something to do with the head
Buttheads butt heads? Or giving head?

butterflies flies that get into the butter

butterflies in the stomach ones that get stuck there and eaten

butterfly effect slight indigestion

cakewalk a dance for ants "Piece of cake!"
Expect *more* insects in the stomach if you eat a piece of the dancehall.

cheapskate a stingy ray

child-bearing enduring unruly kids
In turn, no child can bear its parents. This is a well-established biological law.

a Christian heart Roman Colosseum debris

chronic fatigue syndrome always dressing like Castro

clean and jerk The Odd Couple *(or just Felix)*

clothes hamper nudist slogan

coffee cake A spot of water got into the instant jar.
You can't have your cake and drink it too.

colonist me::!

come from behind something found in gay men's faeces

complement to fit together intimately, as the complementary strands in the DNA double helix; for example,
"I'd like to complement you on your lovely bed."

crosswords
"Get me down from this damned thing," said Jesus crossly.

cyclotron a collide-o-scope of strangely beautiful patterns

couched potato

dateline

1. Middle East food queue
2. "May I buy you a drink?"

International Date Line
"May I buy you a Middle East snack and change your day?"

debris the anti-Semitic rite of replacing circumcised foreskins

digitalis a debilitating disease of computer programmers; viz, impaired use of digits and delusions of becoming a foxglove

Doctor of Philosophy a license for dispensing physics and metaphysics

Doctor of Theology a license for doctorin' doctrine

double-cross The chicken returns.

And well you might ask, why did the chicken double-cross the road?

Dragnet Dumped, a *dumb* dumb.

draw a bath Okay, [- - - -].

drawers where the family jewels are stashed

(until drawn on)

The chancellor has announced new plans for shortening the dole queues. He's asking the men to stand closer together. — *Ronnie Barker*

The early bird gets the worm.
Archaeopteryx gets a parasite and becomes extinct.

earth lover an outdoor type who never bathes

eat and run get diarrhea after a meal; aka **the bum's rush**

Edification teaching a horse to talk (on Ed TV)

endomorphic rock

El Niño the bad guy in a TexMex movie, Billy El Niño (just kidding)

errand making a mistake for someone else

escape clause
Overworked elves break free of Santa the slavedriver.
"That's *sleigh* driver!" (Where'd the elves come from anyhow? Did the Clauses have recessive genes for dwarfism? Or is *she* an elf? Is that why they had to hide away at the Pole? Or was that just so they could practice slavery?)

feel like a million dollars flat, dry, funny colour, piles

fly fishing trying to get it out of your drink before it gets drunk
(A bar fly?)

flying colours kindergarten melee
flying saucers kitchen melee

fool around (He won't leave!)

free range eggs eggs allowed to go anywhere they please

fork **spoon** **scissor** **Freudian slip**

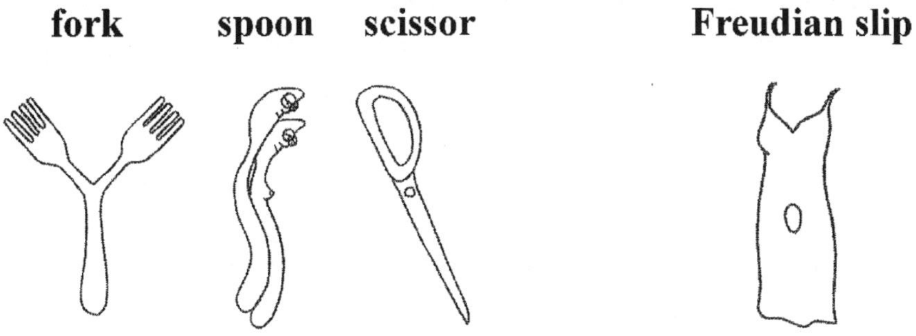

future shock fucked in the ahead

gene pool a game where men get two balls and women get the rest Thanks to Robert McGough.

[He] entered the gene pool while the lifeguard wasn't watching. — *Anon.*

goes without saying secretly dirties one's pants
goes all the way ditto, while rushing to the toilet

go off half-cocked a botched circumcision *(De-bris!)*

go to the wall miss the door

grave robbers thieves with no sense of humour

greenbacks illegal immigrants from Mars
green thumb body part from a UFO crash
"Another damned greenback! Stay home, you freaks!!"

half-breed get half-pregnant

have it all over one fall into a manure pile

head case (o o)
an anatomical enclosure made *out of one's skull* |=|

Nut case: a cracked shell. — *Anon.*

head in the clouds the "mile high club"

Hands up!

hummingbird doesn't know the lyrics

ineffable foolproof,
can't be effed up

in each other's pocket

interest-free loan
a boring book from the library

in the worst sort of way
the dumbest possible approach
Fawlty Towers?
Worst way—left! (anagram)
Just *left?*
Yes, the opposite of *just right.*

jump down one's throat how frogs get there (And hoarses?)

KFC a great place to meet chicks
But would you want your child to marry one?

laugh off have an orgasmic guffaw

laundromat a forum for airing your dirty linen in public

left behind a half ass (The other half is **right behind**.)

half ass **ass whole**

legless
1. a beetle that disobeyed its mother and played with the giant kid
2. a kid that disobeyed its mother and played with the giant bottle

life "the scum of the earth"—a thin green film on a wet rock

life, the secret of Due to limited space, this item could not be fitted in. Apologies. Please check a later edition.

listless having no agenda

PHYSICS AND SOCIETY

line of force "Stop in the name of the law!"
line of least resistance "Certainly, Officer."

loaf behave like a lump of bread

long john silver what a cool klepto wares home from a hotel

low level violence hitting below the belt

macromolecule a large small
majorette a small large
chief petty officer a big little
white dwarf star a little big
(or actor Michael Dunn)

May the force be with you.
I hope the police arrest you.

metamorphic rock
music that changes you
(into a cockroach?)

musical saw

(I tried this. It ate my violin.)

mind your own business be toilet trained

microprocessors tiny pixies who serve summonses, prepare tiny amounts of food, run computers and serve as screen lords

pixel the domain of an individual screen lord pixie

mixed drinks took another's by mishtake (+_+) {(_(}

mountaineers

how the hills hear the sound of music and come alive

mystery tour initiation into an occult cult culture

nanotechnology how Mork got here from Ork

newt a unit of gravity equal in mass to 1 aquatic salamander; named after **Sir Isaac Newt**

night stand an item that traditionally comes in groups of one in groups of two

not your cup of tea
It's the person's next to you!

```
      { -_- }     {!c! }
 _U?    _U?\      | 0 /
```

nuptial mass total weight of the couple including the fetus

nuts and bolts insane asylum escapes

occasional drinker I only drink on special occasions.
Such as a famous person's birthday. Any famous person.

off and running A contradiction—it can't be both.
Yes it can. My watch for example. —Ed.

old boy network a gay seniors' dating service, **ob-scene.com**

Once a ___, always a ___. The blank never learn.

overdrive a feature of lemmings' cars

overland come down with a thud

overturn rectify: 1. > turn 360°
2. rectal intercourse
—for the "**over**"-**sexed**

panic button the one holding up your pants

peas and hominy a balanced, calming diet

peer pressure a full bladder

personify treat a pet as if human—even if you're not

perversity a reform school of higher learning ie, prison

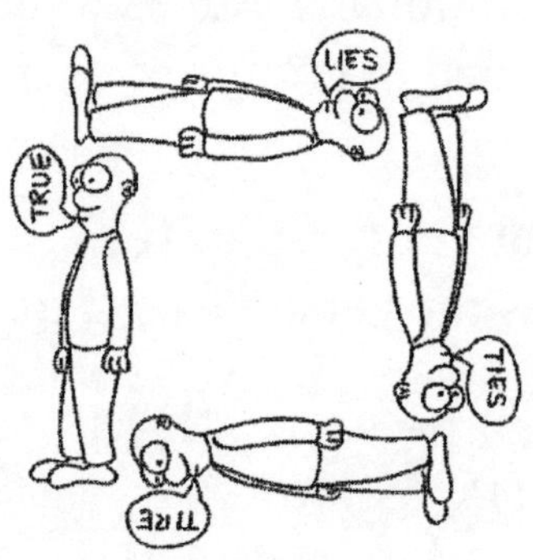

If you lie at the right angles four times you wind up telling the truth.

We're going to turn this team around 360 degrees.— Jason Kidd

What must a horse think after a race is over? "We were just here. What's the point of that?"
— Jerry Seinfeld

phallic symbol a psychological crotch (the shape of things to come)

physics
They work out the deep shit.

pinballs, pinpricks, pinholes
genitalia of the common pin

pipe dream to marry a lovely cigarette holder and raise fags

play cat and mouse
sleep and eat cheese

pied piper

picking one's brain

play on words a silverfish drama in the dictionary

point-blank no bottom line *(I don't get it. — Ed.)*

point your finger put it in the pencil sharpener

poke a slow punch
Not necessarily alcoholic, it may come from a cow.

polymorph to turn into a parrot

polyphony Monty Python's parrot

prefab before you were wonderful

preferable In the US *pref*erable is preferable to pre*fer*able; in the UK *pref*rable is preferable to *pref*erable or pre*fer*able; in Australia no one gives a shit.

pregnant with meaning
having a baby as a philosophical experience
I should know. But I don't.

a price on his head the Mad Hatter

private investigators gynecologists and urologists

A Portrait of the Artist as a Pun Man

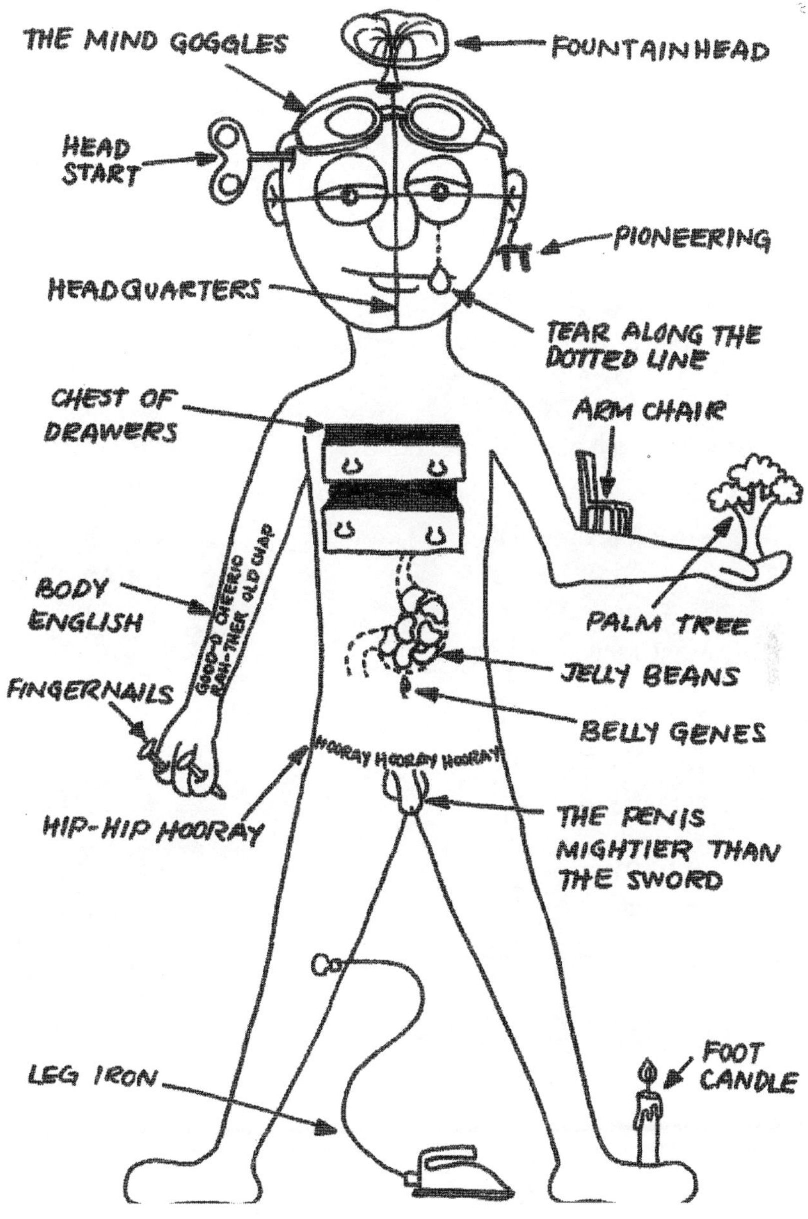

Prince Charming kissing a frog

I had a pet frog once, I named it Charming Prince.
It may have been enchanted but at kissing it I'd wince.
I mean, who wants a prince to take care of?

You can't have everything. Where would you put it? — *Steven Wright*

proctology the end as an end in itself
proctor contraction of prat doctor

propose ask a supermodel to work for you (They work for me.)

psychological abuse thinking off
If physical self-abuse isn't possible, eg in a fox-hole, where foxy supermodel thoughts must do.

protoplasm
that yucky goo on the bottom of the evolutionary ladder

puddle past tense of piddle

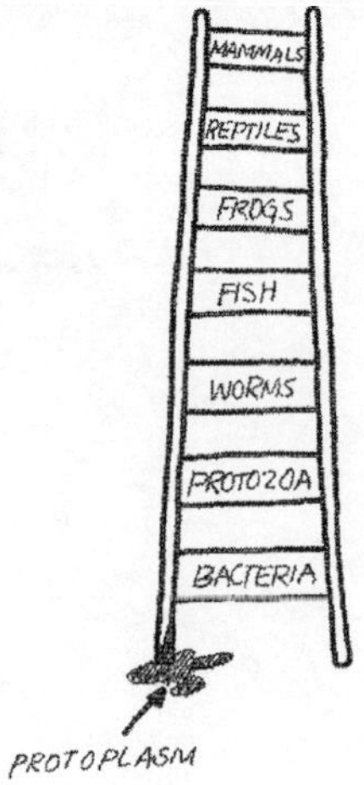

punch line "Take that!"

quickie a baby
(or how to make one)
pinkie a communist baby

[There are] two classes of pedestrian—
the quick and the dead. — *Lord Dewar*

ragout
a stew with the dishcloth removed

racketeer a loud tennis player

eg, McEnroe, Seles, Sharapova, and lately most of them, in the spirit of everything else getting noisier all the time.

racketeers noisy bacterial crims living high on the catgut

rake a "thing" that gathers
fallen flowers and leaves
no forwarding address

recur to have puppies *(Not again!)*

recurring dream

put on shoes and socks

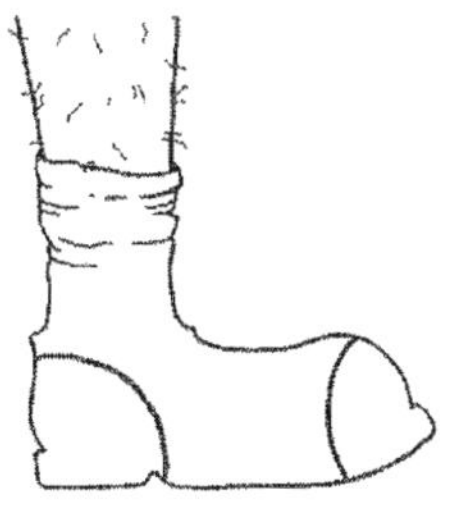

Wrong! Socks first.

(unless on an icy path, says a 2010 Ig Nobel prizewinner)

ram male with a big butt
ramparts encounters male with a bigger butt—and parts

a real brick of the community the village idiot
This is a thick joke. And I must apologise on behalf of my self for using it.

reggae the music of Jah, Maker

reproductive biologist an exspurt endeavouring to make sex understandable to the man in the street: "Sex, you may recoil, intermingles genes. Sex without DNA mixing is inconceivable."

retrospection

seeing eye to eye the intrafacial romance of a crosseyed person; "**an eye for an eye**"

LOVE AT FIRST SIGHT?

selling like hot cakes using a fence

shotgun wedding

sitting duck

If you ducked in time you're <u>quick</u>. You show <u>presence of mind.</u>

sexual intercourse an activity where the penis gets out of hand
"One thing led into another."

The shoe is on the other foot. So *that*'s where it went!

shooting pains "Hey, mate, that bullet really hurt!"

stand in fail to notice it was there
wet behind the ears up to your ears in it
up to your ears in it up to your eyeballs in it
(Inspired by *Australia, You're Standing In It,* classic '80s comedy series.)

stand-up comedy nice work if they can get it (Get it?)

the taste of fear tastes like chicken

That'll be the day. what hillbillies say at dawn
Done up. what they say when pestered to wake up

tickling the ivories foreplay in elephants
tickled pink foreplay in pink elephants

torture chamber music four rank amateurs playing a Mozart quartet in your home as a gift from great-uncle Otto

"Do you play the violin?" "I don't know, I never tried." — *Anon.*

a stable diet hay and oats **a staple diet**

time flies
SF insects from the future
Accidentally brought here by
Vincent Price or Jeff Goldblum?

A centrefold? (Laugh-In)

time off for good behaviour
taking a break from bad behaviour

umbrella a magic wand for controlling the weather via
the unbrella effect: "On iffy days, carrying an umbrella prevents rain while leaving it at home evokes rain."

The rain it falleth on the just
And also on the unjust fella,
But chiefly on the just because
The unjust steals the just's umbrella.
— Lord Bowen

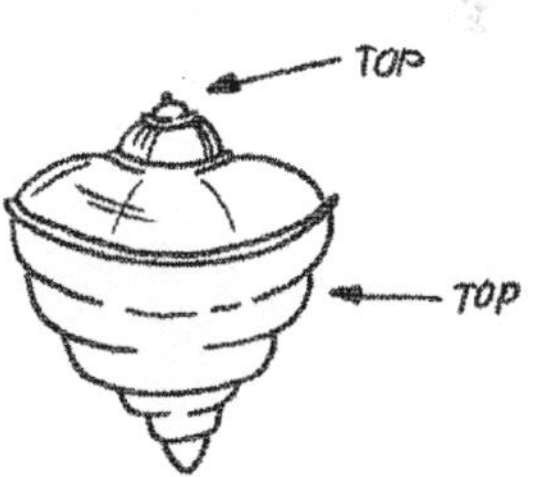

virgin olive oil
before she met popeye

the wheel a revolutionary invention
(It's been round for a long time.)

wouldn't harm a flea a bogus insecticide
bogus = 0 bugs (anagrams; synonyms here but antonyms usually)

tilting at windmills

Your days are numbered. You're on the pill.

(Is it that harmful?)

zero tolerance

1. putting up with the illogical fact that zero is a number
2. tolerating "zeroes", people of no significance

(I would tolerate them if I could find any!)

The final **word** in Pundemonium below is, appropriately, a daring exploration into the very origins of the pun itself. I suspect this is exactly what *Samuel Beckett* meant by *"In the beginning was the pun."* The pun and the word arose simultaneously out of the same bird, as coopposites in the mental dialectic.

word an evolutionary development that grew out of a worm in Adam's apple

In the beginning was the worm.

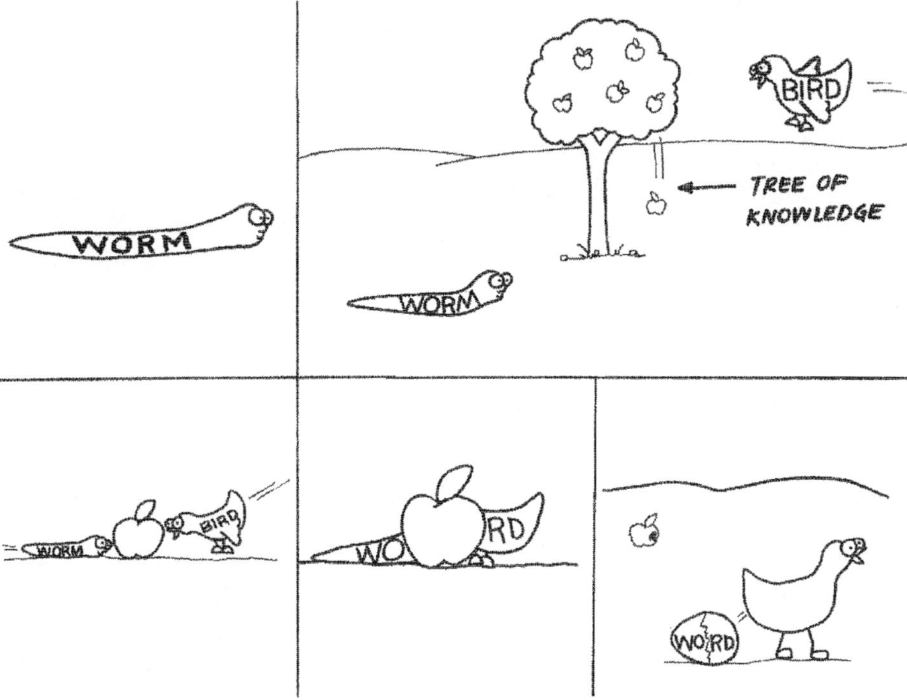

Chapter 2. **CONFUSIONS SAY**

To err is humour. — Anon.

No cow's like a horse, ...no horse like a cow. That's one similarity anyhow.
— Piet Hein

It is impossible to make anything foolproof because fools are so ingenious.
— H. W. Robinson

He [Ronald Reagan] thinks arms control is some form of deodorant.
— Pat Schroeder

A sexagenarian? At his *age? That's disgusting.* *— Gracie Allen*

Clergyman A: *"When I preach I have the congregation glued to their seats."*
Clergyman B: *"Now why didn't I think of that!"* *— Anon.*

This fictionary is a comedy of errors, or wrongisms. In a word, it's dumb. (Apologies if you're dumb, but if so you oughtn't be reading this!) It treats English as the bizarre foreign language it so often is, defining words and idioms as a confused learner might. I mean no disrespect to foreigners either (I'm one myself) or learners (ditto) or the dyslexic (dotti) or other minorities (ditto). I'm not poking fun at them but rather at our wonderfully ambiguous language when looked at out of context. The 'definitions' below are humble and tentative, not answers but questions. "Does that mean this?" This humility is often returned in kind by my post-mortems (in contrasting type) which politely strive to redeem the confused critters by twisting their words back into a reconciliation with standard usage. The things I do for them! They're like children.

above the law

Is this where the term piggyback comes from?

anti-aircraft The attitude of a Luddite? Yes, **jet repulsion**.

artificial intelligence Cheating on exams?

babysitter A child too young to stand?
That's too often the escaping parents' opinion.

bastard file A list of enemies? "The Abrasive Bunch"

beastlike Animal love? How childlike.
childlike Paedophilia? How beastlike!

"Paedophiles" is a bit impartial for my liking: it makes it sound a harmless hobby such as stamp collecting or liking France, and it gets paediatricians' houses burned down, which is bad. — *Julie Burchill*

Big Brother is watching. Emergency babysitter?

blemish Blem-like? Problemish.

blood alcohol concentration Focus on getting drunk?

blood count Dracula? He counts on blood.

bossa nova Tell a stellar explosion what to do?
I doubt if this is actually possible. Perhaps if you hum a few bars.

booby trap how many a man gets snared

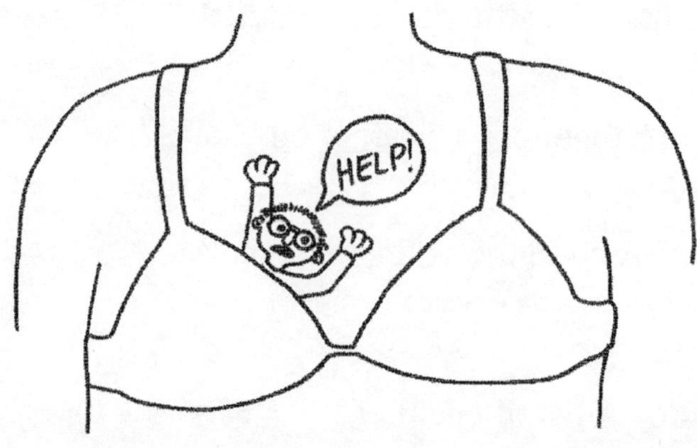

bottled up nerves Had stiff drinks before asking the girls out?

bottom line Cellulite? It is indeed for vain middle-aged women.

carbide A parking lot? (Union carbide is one at Labor headquarters.)

carnal knowledge The field of anatomy?
Yes, especially the juicy bits in the field.

Cartesian section How mathematicians have babies?

cattle crossing Making a bull see red?
Bovine road rage? But why did the road cross the bull?

CD-ROM A Hindu chant? Yes, the chant of the Indian IT industry.

cheep cheep Cry of a bargain-hunter? A chick, no doubt.

cinema complex A fear of movies? Or of too many choices.

closed shop The only one around when you need cigarettes?

cocksucker An easily fooled rooster? Or a fowl parasite?

codpiece A fisherman's lunch? A gay old salt.
codswallop A fish punch? To the codpiece—that's why it's worn.

circus barker

cowboys Interspecies hybrids?
...from the Old West, where men were men and cows were horny

Dartmouth A fast talker? probly a standing Ivy League joke

daughter cells Suite of locked soundproof cellars in Austria?

daybreak Lunch hour? That's about when I usually finish waking up.

decode A ten-line poem?
It's the latest new Espionage Art form, the **cryptode**.

degreed To remove mankind's worst fault? What? PhDs?

denigration and dissemination Hitler's pogrom program to clear the nation of negroes and semites?
A "dis-Semite" nation is a Dis' semi-nation, only half a nation, run by the Devil.

deodorant A lover of God? Deo in Excelsior, as Thurber might've said.

departmental Be driven (away) crazy? by office politics

diagnostic Not sure if Jehovah *or* Allah exists?

dismissing A sex change? Or dropping one's girlfriend?

diversity A school offering two courses? "Two *different* courses!!"

double-check Going Dutch?

dragonfly A giant zipper? Yes, a large insect that zips around.

dress up A cancan dancer? They do wear fancy clothes.

drug abuse Not protecting it from the elements?
like the element of overuse

dog paddle ...**dog paddle** ...**dog paddle**

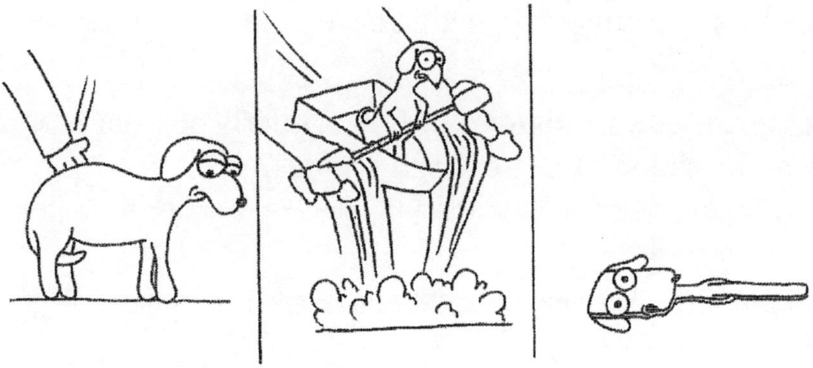

dumbfound Failed the exam? *Unbelievable!*

easy come, easy go An efficient penis?
constantly losing its belongings

ONE
NEO
EON!

eonism The philosophy of our eon?
Could be. The anysex movement.

fair weather friend One who brightens your day?

flat as a pancake A gingerbread apartment?
flat broke Apartment-trained?
Trained not to eat the gingerbread even when penniless.

free speech No honorarium? So you can say anything you like!

eat like a horse

eat like a bird

exorcising a demon

Thanks to Gilly Jordan for exorcising me.

funny as a crutch Uplifting humour? *Not funny!*

getting ahead of yourself

1. Cure for being beside yourself?
2. Split-second time travel?

He's very fast and if he gets a yard ahead of himself, nobody will catch him.
— Bobby Robson

handyman A redundancy?

"Men are those creatures with two legs and eight hands."
— Jayne Mansfield

getting one's shit together Constipation?

Right! The root meaning of constipation is tightly pressed together.

giddy up Vertigo? Or sudden-standing syndrome?

Or first time on a horse?

groovy In a rut?

A pot hole maybe?

grounds for divorce Really bad coffee?
(It happens!)

half-obscenities Two-letter words?
Ay, as "Pp!" or "Go do do!" or "Go *in* it!" or "Up 'er!" or "Up ye, bo!"

heart of gold Fort Knox?
Heart of gold? Ha! I asked them for some once and all I got was a funny look. And the attention of some nearby guards.

helping out
The social responsibility of the bouncer?

hide like an elephant
Behind a lamppost?

Hitting the nail on the head?

This won't damage your brain, for doing it proves you didn't have one to begin with.

holding company
Hugging your visitors?

honest as the day is long
Only cheats at night?

hitting the road

home stretch

humanitarian A cannibal? Too humane to eat animals or vegetables.

ill at ease A workaholic?

infest Inner joy? Yes, an **infestival** for the parasites.

just in time Eventually treated fairly?

lateral thinking "Side effect" of a bent mind?
Bent half the way around to backward thinking?

laughed out of court
Privately found the justice system a joke?

level-headed Bubble-brained?

look like a new person Have a baby face?

Love thy neighbour as thyself. Masturbate them?
Charity begins next door if you live alone.

made to order Forced into command? a custom-made oxymoron

make headway Leave a hole in the top as you knit a sweater?

a male trapped inside a female body Doglock?

low wit Barnyard humour? **To moo "moo mot"?**

mess around Food in the vicinity? Don't play with it!
monkey about A zoo escapee in the vicinity? Don't play with it!

meretricious Deserving praise?
Non-gays also make this **gaud-awful** mistake!

mobile phones

moment of truth A brief pause in the flow of lies?

Mosaic Law
Patchwork legislation?
Patched-up stone tablet fragments.

mummified Pregnant?

name-calling Taking roll?
"...that bastard Ned Adams" "Present"; "that slut Joy Ames" "Present" ...

musical chairs

nanny goat A farmer's babysitter? She sits on the baby.

Never mind. Always disobey?
Mom was all time telling me I never mind.
"... never mind," I'd echo.

nick of time

A burglar alarm?

nightjar A faulty alarm clock?
But not a cuckoo.

nominal value The importance of having a name? a "face" value

off one's face Quickly turn the head pretending not to be staring?
Or pretending one isn't intoxicated.

on and off A quickie?
But only now and then.

on the side of the angels Wings? —and Paul McCartney!

orders or magnitude
Like when Jesus ordered fish and chips for five thousand?

ordure A small snack served at parties?
Seems like it sometimes. Yuk.

organ grinder A biochemist?
Ah, the music! The chug, the squish, the grind! (We were monkeys aspiring to become biochemists long before we were organ grinding biochemistry slaves.)

original sin Creative misbehaviour? Yes, *Creation* misbehaviour.

orology Alternative science?
Making mountains out of molehills? Or building mountains of data against eitherology.

out of one's depth Where faeces come from?
Yes! Superficial humanshit.

packhorse A horse with a huge souvenir collection?
It can't say neigh to any load of crap.

palm off Masturbate? Well, you can always palm it off as safe sex.

paperweight A very light category of boxer?
But don't let one hit you in the temple. Or in the office for that matter.

parting shot

Nearly a de-parting shot.

pass out Distribute literature?
And faint when you finally read it?

peepshow The chick tent at the state fair?
"Watch naked chicks emerge from shells!"

penny dreadful Fear of change?

penthouse One that's bottled up?
Yes, for parties.

periscope Mouthwash for fairies?
Scope™ is popular on submarines, where bad breath can cause real problems.

pie in the sky A free lunch?
...falling from an airplane?

pink elephant A cocktail? ...too many.

in the pipeline

playboy An inflatable male for lonely women?
Yes, Hugh Hefner for example.

plum loco Home grown fruit? -cake

poppycock The limp member of an opiate user? *Nonsense!*

press charges Reporters rush celebrities? who have them arrested

priggery Where prigs are kept and bred? "*Well* bred, mind you."

private parts Roles in home movies? Naughty ones of course.

proctology The science of monitoring exams?

Yes, exams of anuses—or by anuses, depending on one's side of the anus. (Anus is a medical euphemism here.)

process of elimination An act so rude it is confined to closets?

You looked for a toilet in every other room.

public relations The ones you don't mind admitting to?

pull off Isn't that something that's *not on*?

Not if you can pull it off. Just don't pull it *off!*

pundits Jokewriters who gang up and rob books?

BAN PUNDITS—PUN BANDITS!

pothead

Do you prefer grass or Astroturf?

Tug McGraw (baseballer):

I dunno. I never smoked Astroturf.

— *DimWit*

quandary

Where rocks are mined?

...or minds are rocked.

the quick and the dead Manicure jargon?

rolling in the aisles Making cigarettes at the movies?

Funny cigarettes, curled up in laughter?

record sleeve

salad days A crash diet?
Make every day a **hayday**, hey?

screwing boring *What??*

second hand watch
Counting down to midnight?

send up the river Ridicule it?
"What are you forever running away from, you silly river? Prison?"

sentence A declaration followed by a period? a period up the river

the short end of the stick The one nearest the opposite end?

> *I told you to make one longer than the other and instead you made one shorter than the other.* — *Sir Boyle Roche*

skin flick The final step in circumcision?

sleep tight Prelude to a hangover?

splitting headache
1. A headache that is mercifully leaving?
2. A headache shared between two? Parenting, for example.

First half of #2 is from a 1940s *Ramar of the Jungle* serial.

tongue in cheek Ooo, is this an unmentionable perversion?
Like "prick up your ears"? No, it's a French kiss, Filthhead. (Just kidding.)

shortening bread

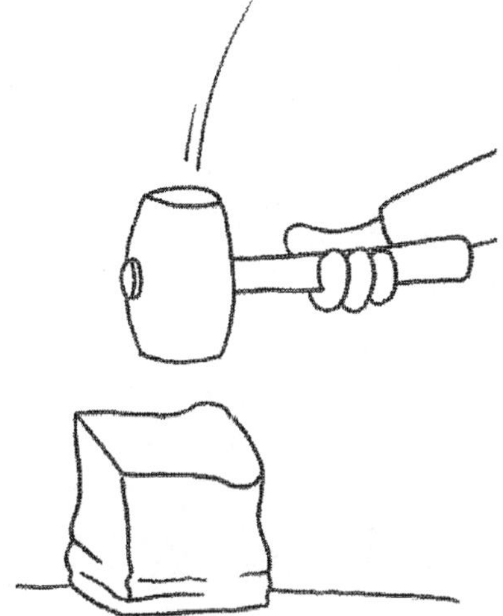

speaking with a forked tongue

tap dancing

swan dive

V8 race

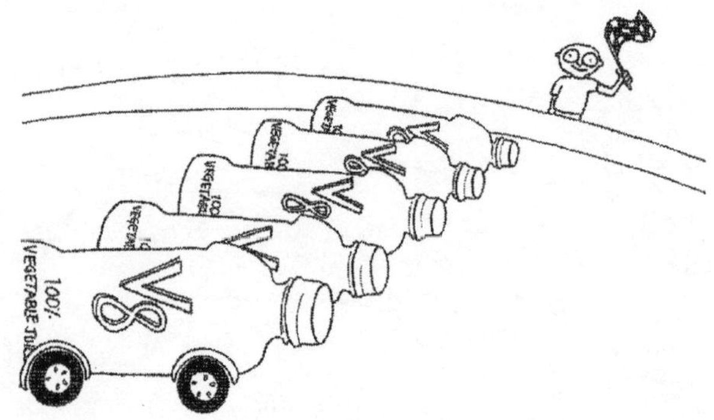

talking through one's hat

wearing more than one hat

hat trick

Thanks to Jasmine for hat trick.

travelling on a shoestring

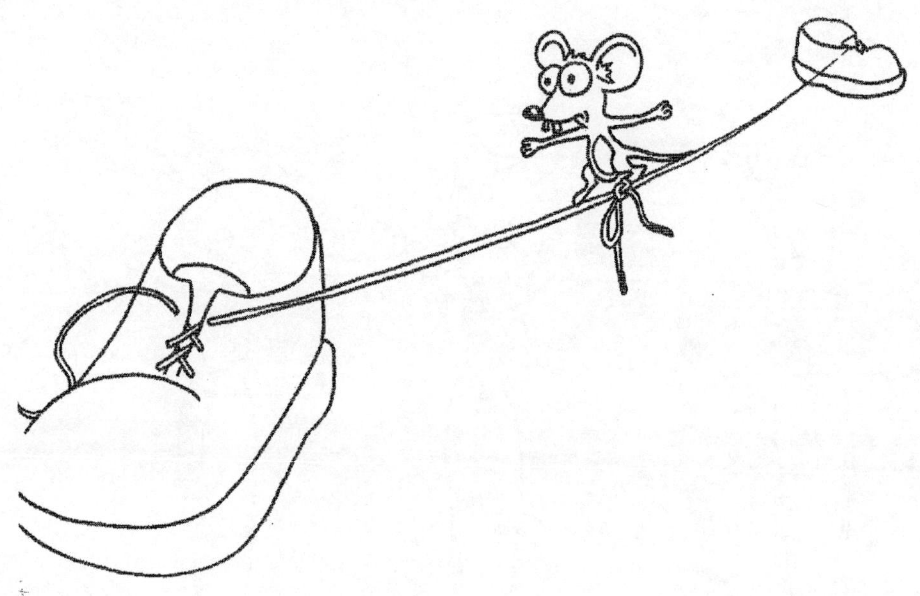

under oath
Swear less than usual?

underpants
Doesn't breathe deeply enough?
Are his briefs too brief?

up to scratch
Why the dog got out of bed?

vote with your feet
Use the handicapped booth?

well off
Good riddance?
I'm made richer by your absence.

What goes around comes around.
Isn't this a circular argument?
Yes, like much of this book.

up tight

Chapter 3. **BIBLIOFILE**

I learned about sex the hard way—from books. — *Emo Philips*

If you drop a Bible on a field mouse, it'll kill it. So maybe the Bible's not all good. — *Harry Hill*

When thou has made an end of reading this book, ...thou shalt bind a stone to it, and cast it into the midst of Euphrates... — *Jeremiah 51:63*
(Just try not to hit any field mice.)

The love of books can drive one to strange behaviour such as forever making lists of them. That's me. Part 1 is a list of those I've breathed from. Part 2 is a sneak preview of books I'll be writing or finishing in the future. Assuming I live to be 1000 as I've always expected. Look to your laurels, Methuselah!

Thanks to Sue for "bibliofile".

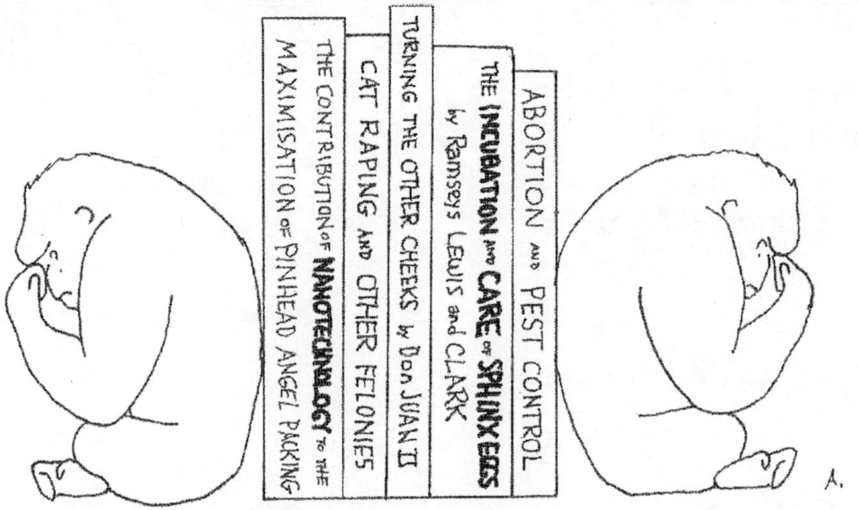

Chapter 3, Part 1. **BOOKS DRAWN ON**

In putting together all the unholy mixes in the *How to Double the Meaning of Life* play, I have drawn on the following books. I paid for it too with a hefty fine for defacing library property. They wouldn't buy the argument that my drawings actually enhanced the value of the books.

A. **Institutionalised Publications**

My primary source has been one of the Church's ***Complete Completeness*** titles,
A Complete Cross-Indexed Catalogue of Possible Absurdities
(*Abridged Thirty-Nine Volume Edition)* I was denied access to the unabridged! Just because they think I'm the Anti-Christ or some such flimsy excuse?

I've also been inspired or amazed by this companion pair of Church publications:
Eschatology Archives: Questions to Ask God on Judgement Day
Scatology Archives: The Deep Shit
Eschatology concerns the end process, scatology the end product.

This is a government white paper I intercepted:
National Boredom Week, a Proposal to Increase the Birth Rate

Other unauthorised publications consulted include:

Precedings of the First International Plagiarism Congress
(Actually the Second. — Ed.)

IQ Daily—the Smart Londoner's Shopping Guide, 1932-1967
Great tips on all the bargains worth waiting in line for at the time.

The Plane Truth: Organ of the Flat Earth Society
"A *plane* can take you deeply into the 3D," they argue airily.

An Atomically Correct Universe Kit: The Owner's Manual
Author and publisher unknown.

B. **Scholarly Monographs,** individually authorised

Integration and Disintegration—a Black Mathematician's Drug Guide, by Cosmic Ray Robinson

A Transparency-Illustrated Collection of See-through Ideas, by Marcia and Walter Mellon
Enjoy some of the shallowest thinking you'll ever run into. Rated PG.

Nonsense and Sensitivity, by Jane Autrey
Be glad I read this—it curbed my political incorrectness. *(Not a whole lot. Ed.)*

The next three touch on very coarse matter and only my irrepressible honesty compels me to admit that I consulted them. Reluctantly.
The Whole Dirt Catalog, by Thirty Old Men
Listening with the Third Leg, by Dr. Seymour Feelth
Theoretical Foundations of the Orgy, by "Town Hall" Buckles

But this *Journal of Quantitative Theology* monograph is decently dull.
A Mathematical Approach to Circular Reasoning, by Judge Gduj

The next two neutralised each other and so are hardly worth mentioning.
Textbook of Inspirational Chemistry, by Rev. Timidity-Leery
Medical Ethics Text and Pretext, by Strange Doctorlove

Back from the Grave! by Buzz Offenbach
Rediscovering the Joys of Frivolity.

Fearful Cemetery, by Anne Bigh and Father O'Long
We're scared to death of dying. But to maintain a balance, we're also scared to death of living, or of "not living". So no worries, it's all nicely cemeterical.

Chapter 3, Part 2. **FUTURE TITTLES**

Part I highlighted some of my sourcerers. (^{SOURC}$_{ER}^{E}_{R}^{S}_{?}$) I shall now titillate you by showing you my titties, sorry, tittles—little unfinished or unstarted writings, for posthumous publication if I live long enough to find a publisher at the time.

Parts of the Future Tittles list have been detained in the other four acts in this play and couldn't make it to Act I. My lawyers are trying to secure their release, but we're not hopeful.

My Goodness, An Autobiography
a refreshing rejection of false modesty showing me to be a basically decent bloke

Confessions of a Toothsaver, or Wisdom Once Removed
I thought saving my wisdom teeth would enable me to remain wise. Alas, not. Still, their loss makes a handy dandy excuse for my stupidity.

A Textbook of Pornographic Genetics, or Let's Get Into Each Other's Genes Learn how to set up your own DNA encounter group.

Inner Core Pornography
Over 304 full-colour enlarged photographs of the insides of women's naked vaginae, wombs, tubes—and ovaries! It's *deeply* sexy. Also an aid to prenatal regression.

The Sudden Hemisphere
Oz beckons NH podeans to come here and hang upside down with your hang-up side down. Let the blood and consciousness reach the "southern" hemisphere of your brain. Be surprised at the powers suddenly unleashed.

The Brain Specialist and the Brain Generalist
The thrilling story of a stormy romance between a neurotic neurologist and a psychotic philosopher. I won't reveal the surprise ending at present. Oh, okay. It turns out they're one and the same person. It was all done with mirrors.

Strange Answers to Some Strange Questions

Lost Will and Testicles

The dispirited eunuch left his will in the surgeon's waste. (The penis is called the **willy** because it hangs down like a **y** from those two seats of a man's **will**.)

Higher Learning in Giraffes

Only birds have higher brows than giraffes. We're well down the list.

I Fought the Mighty Roc and Lied to Tell About It

A short tall tale.

Peter Pantheism, the Masculine Perspective

A pubescent boy's fantasy set in his mother's No-Never!-Land, escalating into adult male chauvinism. This story of bell tinkering and hookers is not suitable for mature adults.

Batman, Son of Dracula

A complete genealogy uncovers other bloody or batty ancestors.

Asinine Tales

THE ENDS of Act I

Act II

PANDORA'S DICTIONARY

OPENING UP A WHOLE NEW CAN OF WORDS

earthworn
(six feet under)

The trouble with words is that you never know whose mouths they've been in. — *Dennis Potter*

This Act addresses Potter's dilemma in both positive and negative ways by opening up a can of words in two senses in the two chapters.

Loads of new words, if I may call them that, *free of prior contamination.* I have avoided speaking these virgin words aloud, for your benefit, so they've *never been in any mouth.* (Just in my fatty, yucky, gelatinous brain and on my grubby fingertips.) So you can be the first kid in your neighbourhood to voice them!

Here I justify Potter's phobia by slinging real-word mud in all directions, daggy and daggery. It's a devil's dictionary of satire mixed with ongoing nonsense. Much of chapter 4 is also satirical, you will have noticed.

how the rat race ends
or going round the bend on a bender in the blender

Even if you win the rat-race, you're still a rat. — *Wm. Sloane Coffin*

Part I. **JUST REWORDS**

COINAGE CATALOGUE OF A NEW-MYSTIMIST

Oh Brave New WORD that has such people in it.
— after *William Shakespeare*, who would approve

For of all sad words of tongue or pen,
The saddest are THOSE THAT might have been.
— after *John Greenleaf Whittier*, who might not approve

English is the great vacuum cleaner of languages: it sucks in anything it can get. — *David Crystal*

I'm counting on it, David. (Suckers!)

It's a damn poor mind that can only think of one way to spell a word. — *Andrew Jackson*

Increase your vocabulary collecting coins! Or get famous coining your own words: play ***logodaedaly!*** (*arbitray or capricious word coinage*, an ironic but real dictionary word) Minting coins is a serious crime against seriousness, mind you, so be a lert. But if you just like to watch crime, read on as we move ever **newords**. Some **neoisms** are from *Word Ways*, May '07. Words created by misspellings, like the first up, I dub **Andrews**, after the Jackson quote. Oll Korrect?

abscense a condition in the alleged brain of politicians, a swollen cavity containing pusillanimous matter

academentia a degenerative disease of higher education, part of th genrl dumin dn

adult-proof so complicated only kids can operate it

A child of five could understand this. Someone get me a child of five.
— *Groucho Marx*

anticipatience containing the excitement of great expectations

appear pressure
the need to seem to be as busy as one's co-workers

arkecology the biology, feeding and interaction of the millions of animals crammed into Noah's Ark

ark eulogy memorial praise for the millions of fossil species that died and became extinct on the Ark

CREATIONIST DREAMING

The only thing that stops God sending a second flood is that the first one was useless. — *Nicolas Chamfort*

arrowbiography A chart of one's life designed to illustrate the truism that the best things in life are always in the future when you're young and in the past when you're old. The trick is to recognise that best-time transition point and 'eternalise' it at the time. A typical arrowbiography looks something like this:

... → → → → → → → → → → → → ↑ ← ← ← ← ← ← ← ← ← ← ← ...

I will strive to live each day as if it were my fortieth birthday. — Anon.

assertainty

asso a simple bastard *per se*

atomically correct don't mention Hiroshima or Chernobyl

beat-to-a-pulp fiction violent stories sickos masturbate to

Beer Now the mantra of alcohol-enlightened mystics

bimbus a male bimbo, head in the clouds

blanket verse love poems for the bedroom

bookworn a bookworm who has read enuf books to become frazzled and worn at the edges; **ookwor** in extreme cases
(I'm an **ok**er myself, to get personal.)

boomorangutan
Blowing or throwing the red ape to extinction will come back to **haunt us down**.

brotherfucker incest, or just the latest mock insult

buck rabid a male sex maniac Or is that a redundancy?
anagrams: **Rubba dick, bucka bird.**

Buenos Aryans Nazi refugees to Argentina

capitalist punishment DEATH TO THE UNRICH!
anagram: Capitalist punishment "**spent him**" **'til act is a pun.**

carnival knowledge Fair two meddling
anagram: **naked, crawling love**

cat tonic extreme chill-out for cool cats; antidote to catnip

centimentality keeping unused gadgets because they cost a lot
garbage collector's items saved "antiques" thought valuable

cephalic symbols

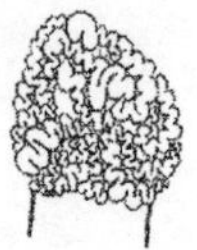
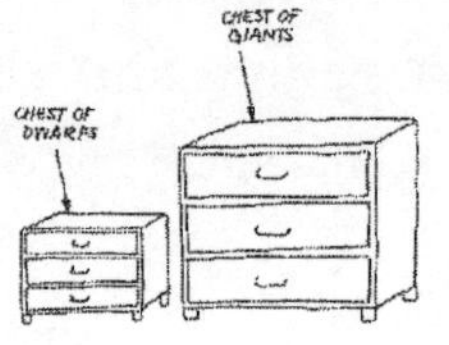

cereal killer 1. too much milk (a well known "Andrew")
2. a genetically modified grain that turns upon humans

Christmass production pumping out millions of figurines of Baby Jesus for the holidays

circumsomnia the Casanova syndrome Ta to John O'Brien.

clockenspiel a clock and bull story about why you're late

the collective unconsciousness
the well-fed egocentric ostrich epidemic
This ostrich anagram also buries its head: **Geocentrics** becoming **eGocentrics.**

comfart relief that's worth apologising for

comprehensile a tail that can hang on everything
apprehensile a tail afraid to hang on anything

Contradictionary Everything I like is contraindicated.

This could serve as an alternative title to most any chapter in *How to Double the Meaning of Life*, but it's mainly here as an excuse to plug my book,

> ***up/dn****, a Dictionary and Contradictionary of Anagrams and Pals*

(2001, Word Ways monograph #5). Get it free online at wordways@butler.edu; hardcopy $US10 from Word Ways, 9144 Aintree Dr, Indianapolis, IN 46250.

constipatriotism getting everyone's shit together, tightly packed

crane assault How to catch a bird by the tale: **Race, salt anus, cast anal ruse.** (anagrams) To be taken with two aspirin and a grain o' salt.

crane ass-salt **assaulted peanut**

crements
food, fed in in in-crements,
fed out in ex-crements

cucumbersome

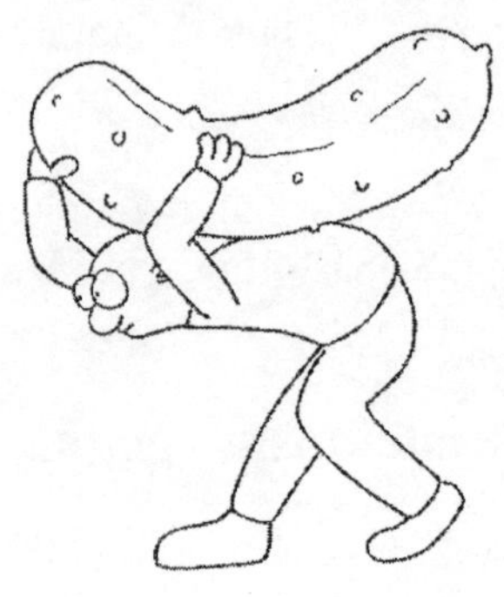

WHAT A PICKLE!

cyanicism a particularly lethal strain of **no-it-all**-ism

danderough (rhymes w/ hiccough)
blowing one's top, a layer of dead scalp

Degas view
the impressionism that you've seen a painting before

demeaning of life making everyone average, or mean

demigoddammit a mild oath

demoncracy a form of government accidentially initiated by a dyslexic President through a spelling errr

He later admitted the war on Iraq was a typo, meant for Iran. Another spelling confusion lumped Koran and Korean into the same axis of evil.

derection "Wither goest thou?" "Came and went."

descent into the mealstream recession blues

The mealstream is the breadline.

ding-ailing sleeping through the alarm—or simply sick of it

disasterisk to remove all footnotes from your writing*

Doctor baiting advanced Master baiting

doledrums the "beat" of the chronically unemployed

ego toenails the lowest form of ingrown conceit

Einsteintaneous faster than the speed of light squared

e-labyrinth

the Internet
dna etacirtni mad
baffling on the god
shtap otni llaf
a person can

empasize feel the pain of the vertically or horizontally challenged

empty nest egg The kids took it and left. — or the financiers!

errmusing funny even when you take a joke the wrong way

eupheminisms nice things said about women in all insincerity

* I do not condone this practice. It's a literary disaster risk.

faecose full of or resembling faeces

I coined this word for those who wish to be erudite and filthy at once. Also available in the less erudite looking US spelling, **fecose**.

faec short for faecose, or a faecose person or thing

I coined this shortening for those who wish to be erudite yet snappy, hip but a touch cryptic, and filthy all at once.

Faec Craec a thing not to get caught up in without a paddle

Faith heeling blindly obeying one's religious leader

> *Faith is closing your eyes and believing with all your might in something you know isn't true.*
> — *Nancy* [and Sluggo] comic strip,'50s (approximate quote)

fastidiots those who swiftly clean up the tiniest mess

> *...so neat she puts paper under the cuckoo clock* — *Henny Youngman*

flauntist
an ostentatious flute player

frisqué perky and suggestive

frogmentation

fruck conceive, have a fruitful fuck

Short for fructify, fruck is more etymologically correct than fuck and should replace it. But will this actually happen? Of course not, nobody gives a fruck.

furiosity obsessive high speed Googling Did furiosity kill the fat?

fourfathers one's great-granddads

Where'd they all come from? I have 2 granddads, 4 great-granddads, 8 great-great-granddads, and so on. If I could trace my ancestry back to Creation in 4004 BC, at say twenty years per generation, I could name 2^{300} male ancestors, or greatly great granddads. There aren't that many atoms in the Universe. Am I being unkind to suspect that my ancestors have a lot of explaining to do on the delicate subject of incest?

gangplan a scheme for mass executions on board by dropping off the end of it

giddy yuppie over-achieving 'cowboy' dizzied by the heights near the top (of the horse?)

ginterpretnig A palindromist trying to interpret something while under the **ginfluence.**

globus interruptus
In the midst of fucking the planet we withdraw just before the climax.

greedhouse effect
Hot air endangers earth life by blocking out effective action.

halfhourglass figure

gymnasties tumbling class stinky-kinky hanky-panky

hemidemisemiquaffer a very very very lite drinker

herewithall Zen alternative to wherewithal

hick hike hokum
A wandering bumpkin's gibberish is Latin unawares.

hopiates drugs of choice for the optimism challenged

hoping mad quasi-clinical insanity from overdosing on same

myopiates antidotes to hopiates, restoring normal healthy shortsightedness and narrowing of expectations

horso

hospitiful one of today's overcrowded, understaffed medical complexes; also spelt **hospitalfull**

howdy duty
In small towns you're expected to say hello to everyone.

humanshit Animal Lib term replaceing bullshit, horseshit, ratshit, chickenshit, titshit, aardvarkshit and other birdturd words equating bad human traits or fruit to animal faeces

ichtheology the belief that God is a fish
This was a view shared by the early Christians.

in broad delight political incorrectness right out in the open

incestors My mom and dad are also my aunt and uncle. We're a close nit family.

Income Poop a financial newsletter for dummies

infeariority anxiety over penis size or breast size

infobia fear of data overload

itchyology the science of fishing for backscratchers
(Combined with ichtheology above, I've confused myself. Now I'll never again be able to spell the term for fish science with any confidence.)

jambore an uninspired jazz session
jamboree one of the disappointed audience members

juke boxing trying to get a recurring tune out of your head
(Definition, but not the coinage, from Barbara Wallraff's *Word Fugitives,* 2006.)

kidunaut a very junior spaceperson Would I lie to you?

knoll coward one afraid to go to Dealey Plaza in Dallas

Latrinity
God, Jesus and Spooks take turns at heavenly toilet duty.

legalitarianism All animals are equal, but some are lawyers.
outlawyers As ignorance of the law is no excuse, nearly all non-lawyers are outlaws.

the life of rile
perpetually angry about falling short of the life of Riley

Macdonna a singing hamburger Now called Old Macdonna.

male chivalrous pig an old style gentlemanly sexist pig

meddle age old enough to know what everyone else should be doing and not doing

megalophobia a *really* large fear of obesity

meremaid The naked lady you saw in the ocean didn't have a fish tail after all.

misdemeaning the petty crime of not getting a joke

mishapiness prone **Miss Happiness prone**

misstressed concrete

Mummies and Deadies common adolescent view of parents

nausoleum a leaky burial chamber for the unembalmed

neighbore a horse that lives next-door and talks a lot but has nothing interesting to say *(Neigh?)*

officialdumb a dense bureaucrat—or the lot collectively

oldfactory abandoned building converted into a nausoleum

NEARVANA

(It's not some far away heaven—you're surrounding it!)

opossumism playing dead, a self-neutralising blend of optimism and pessimism

This advanced form of ostrichism solves the problem of the half full vs. half empty glass by emptying *another* half glass into the first one—and *voila,* the problem vanishes! *(Until half the water evaporates, if I may risk being...)*

overbose carrying talking far too much much too far

Patented Nonsense this book
Punography this book when it gets naughty like the next two:

penile servitude a life sentence for the male of the species

penis from heaven

1. a pious, celibate urinary organ
2. a godsend for the sex-starved
3. a personal Godsend for Mary (Don't say in shock horror that God doesn't have a penis. He made "*man* in His own image,...after His likeness".)

penultimatum to write a threat *"This is my next-to-last warning!"*

peter rabbi a circumciser (A "curtailed" rabbit?)

polka dot com website on Polish dancing

posthumorous a joke everyone's already heard

precurser forerunner of the goddam mouse

podeans Northern Hemispherians—or, to us antipodeans, the counter-clockwise crowd

clock wise having the wisdom that makes the world go round the south pole—a wisdom that passeth podean understanding

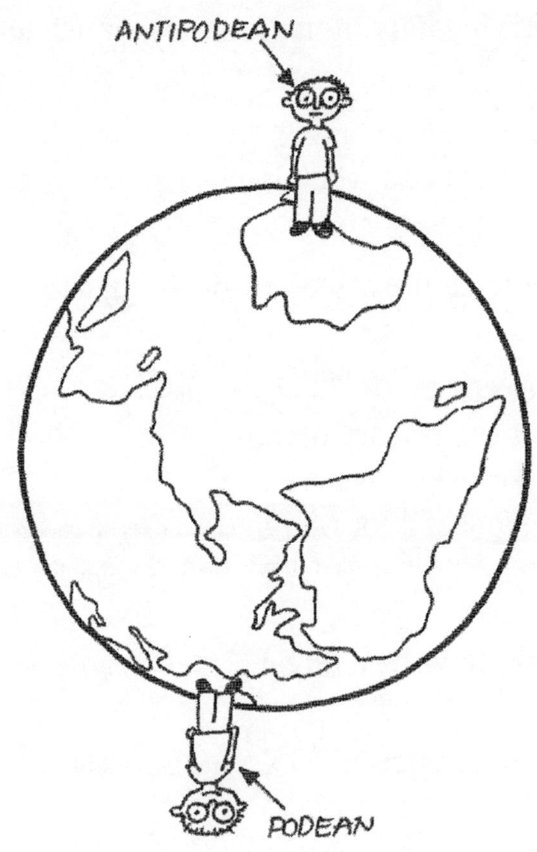

EUROPE SIDE DOWN globe courtesy of New Globe Order

prejuiced I got drunk just to help prove I was right all along.

prophylactic shock an unwanted pregnancy

prospertution getting rich by selling out one's principles

psychobible 1. the **holy strictures** of pop psychology
2. a manual for serial killers

psychopathic doily collector a fancier who collects a lot of doilies, cuts them to pieces and starts over This actually happens. It's like bubblewrap-bursting and perforation-tearing obsessions.

pubic holiday a day without sex
I've been on holiday for eons. It's semi-great!

punambiguous
a joke you don't get and might not have got even if you got it

punultimate a gag one gags on and literally dies laughing at
Or is it the one just before that?

puppy government
sons of bitches doing cur's jobs for absentee top dogs

Qantas mechanics experts in the aerial uncertainty principle

quadrillians truly vast numbers of square dancers
cotillions even larger dance gatherings.

qualm a type of bitter fruit
qualmquash a relative of the qualm and also its antidote

quasimodal a style of bell-ringing

quilt feelings sewing circle therapy sessions

rank and foul employers' view of union members

refusillade the "weaponry" of conscientious objectors

rehashish tending to repeat oneself, being stoned

reke out a living
work hard all your life with little to show for it but body odour
pennies from heavin' the wages of same

remissionary
an evangelist who spontaneously recovers from tropical fervor

RepubWicans a GOP faction led by Elmer "W" Fudd

rhapsoda a soft drink for musicians (Rhap musicians?)

roll model a car that has to be pushed

retrosuppose

Retrosuppose, or use "pre" post. (Preposterous!)

By a preposterous coincidence, these three anagrams are also synonyms. 'Pre post' is in fact the etymology of preposterous.

rotary ho a prostitue hired to service a whole stag party

Not necessarily a Rotary or Elks Club. (My dad was an Elk. Mom was a Dear.)

Shitting Bull USA's treaties with its indigines; technically, **mistreaties**, lies used to abuse.

Didjeridon't Australia's lack of treaties with its indigines, colloquially **give-it-a-miss-treaties**—abuse without bothering to lie about it.

sophomoronic knowing whole libraries less than one thinks
anagram: **A sophomoron**—or *Homo sap*, no?

spaced cadets
druggies kicked out of military academy for getting caught

spermhead opposite of egghead

> *What is a highbrow? He is a man who has found something more interesting than women.* — *Edgar Wallace*

spontanenatnops a palindromist trying to be spontaneous

storkage the surcharge for opening a womb

subblurbs the fine print on packaging where the unhealthy ingredients are listed

suberb An outstanding suburb? Or just an illiterate one? Or an individual under the influence of 'erb?
(All three if you know where to go.)

terminalogy the study of famous last words
I've researched this field and found these to be the most frequent last words: *Oops; Oh shit; Aiyee; Ouch, that stings!;* and *You dare me?*

terrafying making a planet earthlike (scared shitless)

theces bullshit or ratshit dissertations *No,* ***humanshit!***

theoretical atheology what God would be like if He existed

When I told the people of Northern Ireland that I was an atheist, a woman in the audience stood up and asked if the God I didn't believe in was Catholic or Protestant. — *Quentin Crisp*

Theosaurus a recently discovered ancient stone book listing all the dinosaurs God excluded from Noah's ark

It disproves the scenario presented earlier under **ark eulogy** that dinosaurs died out *on* the ark, like in the Bible version where the ark embraced pairs of "every living thing". Also contradicting me and the Bible, *Theosaurus* cites an anagram, **kangaroos as ark no-go** (stuck away Down Under). Yet...

By perseverance, the snail reached the Ark. — *Rev. C. H. Spurgeon*

Unfortunately, after all that effort the two snails weren't admitted into the Ark! The reason? They were the same gender. "We're hermaphrodite—both in one!" "Sorry, no go. Opposing pairs only. The *Devil* snuck hermaphroditism, homosexuality, masturbation, group sex and extended families into God's perfectly balanced dualistic Creation." So the snails hitched a ride on the outside of the Ark, like misfits ever since.

tomatom smallest subunit of tomatoness

TOMATOM

You think the opposite of tomato is non-tomato? Not so. They're just two points on the spectrum between absolute nothingness and total tomatoness.

(HIGHLY ENLARGED)

tortous inclined to commit crimes at a turtle's pace

"Aesop's tortoise tortous this trick," said the crooks slowly.

tranquilt Linus's security blanket

transparenthood communal living

tripode epic poem about a journey on a three-legged horse

troglobite a Creationist—a cave-dwelling fossil half a billion years out of touch

Look at this rock God sculpted to look just like a little animal.
What a clown the Creator is!

ub anatomically correct spelling of up; opposite of **qown**

ubisquitous a type of bakery product found everywhere

unbiblical cord a rope drawing one into heresy *From birth?*

underaware not realise your slip is showing or your fly open
rear unawed Anagram and pun; awe-wearness should be taught young.

undermind the source of puns (and what they've done to English!)

unicoronation A pointy-headed fantastical being is 'elected' king by promising a **unicornucopia**. *(or **uni-corny utopia!**)*

uniformation making everyone like everyone else
(But I already like everyone else.) (Well, nearly everyone.)

United Damnations
agenda of the UUAC: the UN Un-UN Activities Committee

unprophetability 1. failure to foresee a bear market coming 2. the tendency for a lost object to reappear just after a replacement has been bought

unsolicit counteract or de-subscribe to unsolicited ads, spam or junk mail in all its forms
Send your name and address and $3000 and I'll tell you how it can actually be done!

veneerly
Only superficially, as in "I veneerly joined the revolution."

veni, vide, 0! Can't find anything of interest in a video store.
vide0 short version of same
These answer another call for *Word Fugitives* (p.126). See "juke boxing" above.

ventriloquium
a conference where dummies speak for themselves
These are quite rare in reality; most dummies speak for someone else.

veteranarian an old pet doctor who's been to war
As a Nazi soldier?

wanky noodle dandy a jerk-off who thinks he's stylish

warfair military conflict between evenly matched sides
a rarely useful word

weekling a seven-day-old baby unable to lift heavy weights

the Westorn World the tattered planet we leave in our wake
Make that "in our sleep".

whodidit a grammatically correct murder mystery

whopping cough a hack loud enuf to wake the neighbours

weirdy hippo
a drop-out river horse into peace&love&sex&drugs&rock&roll

anagrams:
Hippopotamuses' hippo pot amuses.
Pop up moist as he humps a opposite.

widow biddy a shrivelled up little baby-talking granny

wird With 3 pronunciations this is a **weird-wired word.**

wirdo Yours truly, a word-wired weirdo, a revolutionary **wordshipper** prepared to blow the whole dictionary to **wordsmithereens** and propel the pieces into abstract space.

Xenopus complex
a love/guilt relationship with the South African clawed toad

yielled shouted "uncle" very loudly

zoombie (rhymes with die)
one of the undead speeding past, blown up by binoculars

QUICK -FIXES

Here is a special way of making up words: combine prefixes and suffixes with no intervening substantive. Mostly from *Word Ways*, Feb,'06.

A-ism A metaphysical system more modest than *The*-ism or even *A/the*-ism. Basically it's **pan-the-ism**, a denial of all isms. It's derived from the ancient Egyptian religion **Isisism,** which teaches that "Whatever Is Is." A-ism's sacred chant is its anagram "**Am Is!**"
This incantation was later stolen by those young upstarts Kingsley and Martin.

apoistry the art of being elsewhere when needed

deer one who undoes
But a buck deer is one who does.

demimore 1. half an addition
2. nearly an actor

ipseology the study of sameness *(Not again!)*
rely and againly *(Re-ly and true-ly?)*

neoism this word, for one
for **O**ne **N**eo **E**on (A New Age)

retroitis an itchy bum

paratropic drawn earthward when leaping from a parachute
another rarely used word

supraallo almost different

transol the other guy's drink { >,>} u (._.)

Chapter 5.
PROVOCABULARY

An Alphabetical Introduction to
WORD WAR III

Pandora's box

Before declaring war on words and trying to provoke you with *my* vocabulary, first a word from my teachers.

Modern technology
Owes ecology
An apology.
— Alan M. Eddison

Vice
Is nice
But a little virtue
Won't hurt you.
— Felicia Lamport

Satire is simply humour in uniform. — *Paul Jennings*

Satire is a kind of glass, wherein beholders do generally discover everybody's face but their own. — *Jonathan Swift*

Fight air pollution—inhale. — *Red Buttons*

Life in Lubbock Texas taught me two things: One is that God loves you and you are going to burn in hell. The other is that sex is the most awful, filthy thing on earth and you should save it for someone you love.
— *Butch Hancock*

I sometimes think that God, in creating man, somewhat overestimated his ability.
— *Oscar Wilde*

Lunatic in Bedlam: "The world said I was mad. I said the world was mad. And they outvoted me." — *Anon.*

Justice must not only be seen to be done, it must be seen to be believed.
— *J. B. Morton*

Justice is open to all, like the Ritz Hotel. — *Judge James Mathew*

The upper crust is a lot of crumbs held together by dough. — *Anon.*

Conservatives feel they deserve everything they've stolen. — *Mort Sahl*

Maybe they should call themselves **de-servatives**, eh, Mort?

An honest politician is one who when he is bought will stay bought.
— *Simon Cameron*

Let the people think they govern and they will be governed. — *Wm. Penn*

If voting changed anything they would make it illegal. — *Anon.*

Being in politics is like being a football coach. You have to be smart enough to understand the game and stupid enough to think it's important.
— *Eugene McCarthy*

Politics gives guys so much power that they tend to behave badly around women. And I hope I never get into that. — *Bill Clinton*

When I was in third grade, there was a kid running for office. His slogan was, "Vote for me and I'll show you my wee-wee." He won by a landslide.
— *The Golden Girls* (Little Billy Clinton by any chance?)

If God had intended politicians to think, he would have given them brains.
— *Yes, Minister*

Egotism is the anaesthetic that dulls the pain of stupidity. — *Frank Leahy*

That boy will make his way in this country; he has no sense of humour.
— *George Bernard Shaw*

The one serious conviction that a man should have is that nothing is to be taken seriously. — *Samuel Butler*

This President is going to lead us out of this recovery. — *Dan Quayle*

Our enemies are innovative and resourceful, and so are we. They never stop thinking about new ways to harm our country and our people, and neither do we. — *Dubya*

For every fatal shooting, there were roughly three non-fatal shootings. And, folks, this is unacceptable in America. It's just unacceptable. And we're going to do something about it. — *Dubya*

I know how hard it is for you to put food on your family. — *Dubya*

Nothing is more foolish than to talk of frivolous things seriously, but nothing is wittier than to make frivoloties serve serious ends. — Erasmus

Erasmus would love and hate this volume, for opposite reasons. I do both of the above here. It's another fictionary, like act I of this play (*Pun Fun)*, but it mixes serious satire with pseudosatire, wise sayings with wise cracks, intended to highlight rather than cancel each other and to provide some "serious relief" to the relentless corniness of *Pun Fun.* The serious **gnomic puns** were revealed to me by gnomes. You've already run into some in Part I of this act. More are scattered through the remaining acts of *How to Double the Meaning of Life.*

WARNING: Reading some of the following may be hazardous to your health (or mine!) if you're a Right Whinger or any other sort of True Believer.

asteroids | **humanoids**

star piles | earth piles

academic freedom
absence of annoying intellectuals and scary free thought

accountability skill at bookkeeping—a la Enron and Madoff
I've heard Madoff pronounced "mad, off" and "made off". Take your pick.

army surplus overkill

bah what sheep say instead of ruminating over a new idea

Better dead than red.
the attitude of fools who
chronically run stoplights

beginner's bike
"Start simple!"

bite-throat competition
"a more personal approach"

blindfold
the unquestioning congregation
—and what they wear to church

bulletproof use of a gun
to prove one's superiority
"I'm better than you *(bang!)*
—coz I'm still alive!"

capital punishment bankruptcy

brainwashing **brain-twister**

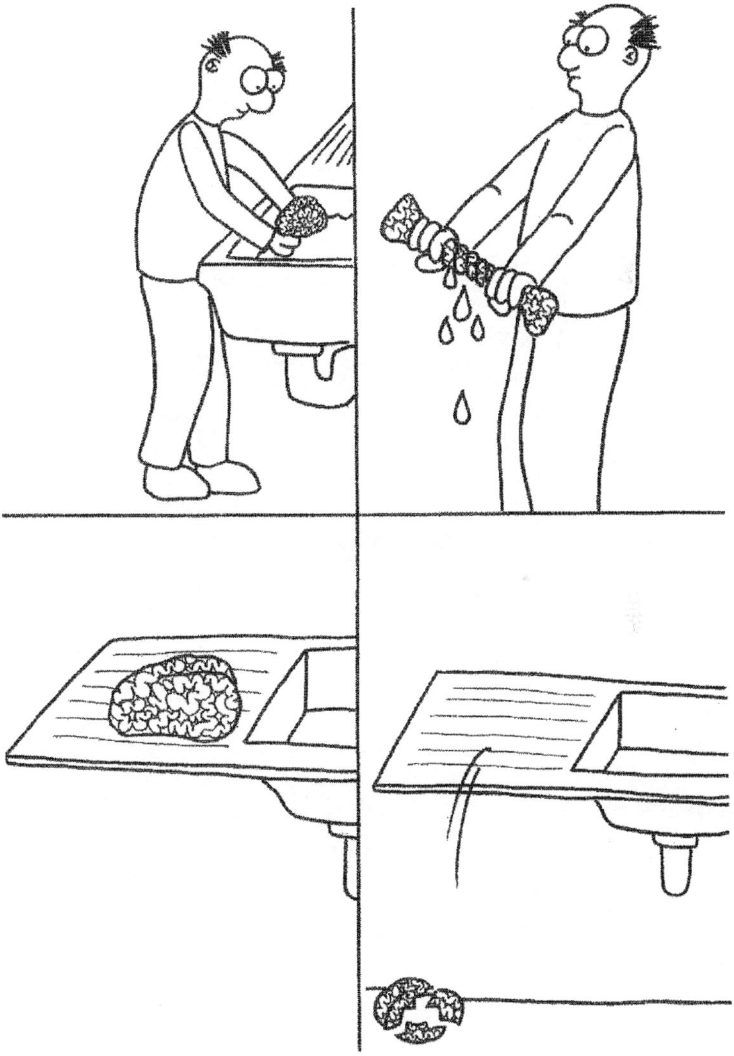

brain drain **brain damage**

bun in the oven

a backward suicide

bushmen primitive Republicans, advocates of the "**primitive strike**"

caterpillers of the community MDs and pharmacists
The catered pills can metamorphose into a butterfly effect.
Note the similarity of **pill**, **pillar**, the obsolete **piller**, to plunder, and **pillage**, the dispensing of pills.

Coalition of the Willing Aus-UK-US
Pronounced "Aw, suck us!" originally; now pronounced "Awe-suck, cuss."

cold turkey trying to give up Kentucky Fried Chicken

colonial just above anal and rectal
colonise Give an irrigating enema to wash out native cultures "because they're shit".

congestion two things digesting each other (a type of marriage)

conservatives slow learners

conspiracy theories too much machination

Cool your heels. Throw the scoundrels into the cooler.
And the modern antithesis,
Kick up your heels. Promote them to the top jobs.

day care Water and feed all its hours.

death duty your obligation not to live forever

degreed (vb) to free of avarice
Ha! Lawyers are degreed.

demonic device a tool to help you forget

discount broker Ignore his advice.

diabetic helpful in two ways
—to the sugar industry and to the health industry

diaper rash the population explosion

No wonder the stork-raven is angry. Will it not end until we run out of storks?

Don't give a darn. Wear holey clothes and a "sew what?" attitude.
Don't give a damn. Don't wear Holy clothes, judge not.

drug lord The Creator

He gave us alcohol, tobacco, cannabis, peyote, magic mushrooms, poppy, coca, cacao, coffee, tea, sugar, cream, etc, etc, etc. Anti-druggies must believe Satan rather than God created the world.

double take

duty-free shopping irresponsible spending

Consumer goods cons 'um, ergo ODs.

eco rat

short for <u>eco</u>nomic <u>rat</u>ionalist and <u>eco</u>logical <u>tra</u>itor at once

They call it rational to burn down one's house for short-term warmth. Better yet, burn down someone else's house.

"If I don't do it someone else will—and be warmer than me."

encyclopedia a huge, multi-volume Papal decree about child abuse, mostly against

exclamation point when it all becomes too much

fair game an animal that doesn't cheat the hunter out of a kill

the fair sex 1. opposite of the unfair sex (feminist opinion)
the fair sex 2. opposite of the great sex (masculinist opinion)

faith healing
being cured of unfounded beliefs It's a miracle!

figure skating
"creative accounting"—with quite a spin to cap it off

firing pin a metal given to redundant workers
firing squad the committee that gives them out
Aka the **chopping board**. Why do you think they're called *execut*ives?

food for thought

fit to be tied marriageable

"...and married the wrong damned aggravatin' one!"

forge ahead Get rich writing bad checks.

Fox terrier Rupert Murdoch, terrierest

He yelps holy terror to sell News. The paperboy *is* the barking dog.

fundamentalists

a people so humourless they'd miss the point of laughing gas

Examples include evangelicals, suicide bombers and auditors.

Get even with. chill out together

Get the creeps. be an unlucky schoolteacher

Get Thee behind me, Satan. Faustian prayer

It's the incantation used by cheaters seeking an unfair backing, the flip side of praying for an unfair backing from God. Except that God is less likely to help.

godliness shamelessly behaving like God

1. Acting like you own the Universe.
2. Acting like the God of the Old Testament—killing those who disobey you, subjecting your friends to severe trials and tribulations and temptations to test their fidelity, inflicting endless torture on the failures. This is in addition to His petty crimes like adultery and graffiti.

the going thing biodiversity

Goodbye, cool world. 
the suicide note of an overheated species

An optimist is someone who thinks the future is uncertain. — Anon.

the great white dope cocaine, heroin, or Dubya

greenback effect ultimate cause of the greenhouse effect
The greenback draws its color from earth's greenery, which gets lighter as the greenback gets darker. (Money generally, not just the US dollar.)

gross domestic product faeces *(Gross joke!)*

groundhog us!

We have met the enemy and he is us. — Pogo (Walt Kelly)

happy medium a love story with a happy middle
"And they lived somewhat happily, for a while."

"**high on life**" *What, plant life?*

Homo sapiens an ape that descended from the evolutionary tree in order to chop it down

hospitable not at all well Indeed, say anti-altruism modernists.

housekeeper one who pays the mortgage on time
A dwindling breed since 2008.

I was 24 and asked to sign for Rangers. Only a balloon would have said no.
— Steven Thompson

hot air balloon

human interest the usury charged on third world debt

We'll never win the war on poverty till all those poor people surrender.
— Rowan & Martin's Laugh-In

They did! The war on poverty is over now. We won! The poor, too weak and battered to resist further, have agreed to die off quietly.

ill treat what doctors do for a living *(Not always! Ed.)*

India rubber Pakistan

Jesus a sage 3000 years ahead of his time

just what the doctor ordered his fourth sports car

keeping her legs crossed
opposite of keeping her fingers crossed

democracy the law of averages
Mediocracy triumphs as it becomes **mediacracy**—rule by the Media.

left and right wingers two types of bird that can't fly
counterrevolution when left and right wingers get stuck at cross purposes in a revolving door

LEFT AND RIGHT WINGERS GET IT TOGETHER

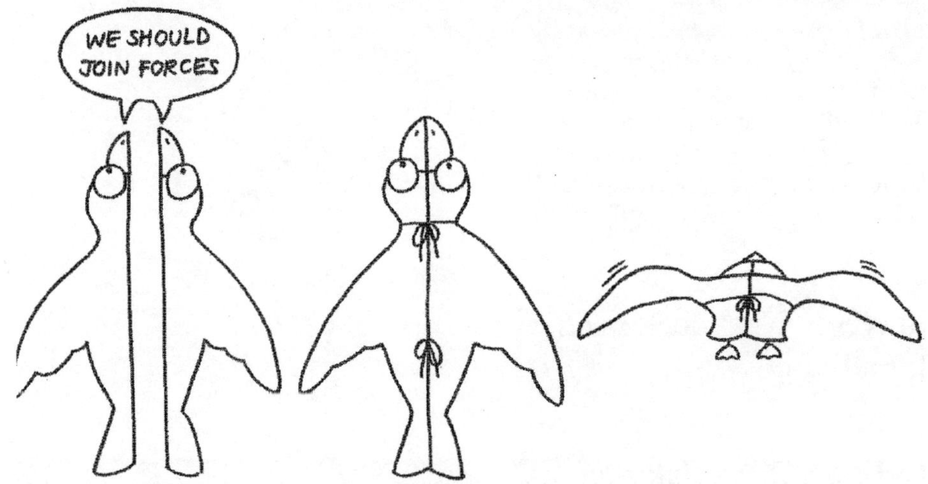

"Why not cut off both extremes and resolve the conflict?" you ask. It won't fly.

liberal (US Media usage) pejorative term for a liberal

life a sentence: a term ending with a period
commonly punctuated by a coma along the way

menses a sentence: a term *beginning* with a period
commonly punctuated by hard labour along the way

local anaesthetic the corner pub

Look on the bright side. how to use a mirror
Look out for yourself.
Stay ever alert for mirrors, now that you know how to use one.

losing your grip a common problem at airports

lowest common denominator a divider posing as a uniter
In politics and marketing it acts as the **low common dominator**.

male outlets female inlets I'm talking electricity here.

mankind an oxymoron?
Yet to be determined. Check back at a later time. If there is one.

mass execution performance of a Catholic ceremony
off the rack Inquisition landfill (from the executed masses)

The Media "where the truth lies" *How uncommonly honest of them.*

military-industrial complex
a personality disorder prevalent in the USA

mind-blowing bursting the seems

money tree policy "Spend money like it grows on trees."

I believe in making the world safe for our children, but not our children's children, because children should not be having sex. — *Jack Handey*

morality play political posturing
moral dilemma
which moral outrage to fake at which time for which crowd

mortgage belt being whacked by your debt (2008?)

motherboard
the panel in China that decides who can have children

narrow-minded hair-brained:
a mind so thin it readily slips through cracks in its reasoning

my brother's keeper

nerve gas $4 a gallon—of all the nerve!

In Oz it's **nerve petrol** at $1.50 a litre, and we're nervous too.

nonsense the only known antidote to sense

Stop making sense. — *Talking Heads*

normal curve a belly-shaped curve (normal these days)

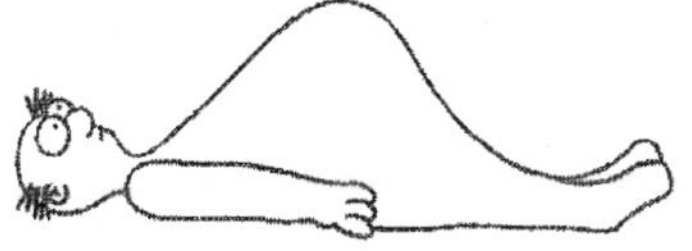

numb drug action
'number' more drug action
...and so are the days of the pothead numbered

Ombudsman a dope dealer—*"but only of cOsMic buds"*
Ombudsperson a politically correct dope dealer

on edge marginalised

on the other hand where the farm worker lays the blame

on the treadmill training to be a hamster

optimism
seeing the glass as half domestic rather than half foreign owned

optimist one who can improve your vision spectacularly.

otherwise a busybody

overhanging leaving the person up too long (a form of overkill)
overkill to hang one person (a form of overhanging)

paddle your own canoe punish it for misbehaving It happens!

pan-Americanism "Yanqui go home!"
This slogan is still heard throughout the Americas, including the southern US.

passive bigotry a contagious disease afflicting the naive

OUTLAW BIGOTRY IN PUBLIC PLACES!

peace the boring bits between wars

hold your peace Contain your tranquility and join the war!

peace offering a bribe to a peace officer

If you don't happen to want peace just say "Peace off!"

pencil sharpener a revolutionary invention

It was necessitated by our no longer having time to whittle away. It's now been superseded by the computer, like everything else that ever existed before.

perseverance

working long and hard toward your ultimate severance

personnel carrier

the one person in the office who does all the work

pharmaceutical industry drug-assisted hard work or sports

play the game go hunting with Dick Cheney

...and play the fool

ploughshares

sword-making material squandered on farming

Plutocracy government by dogs

I know, I know, Pluto is no longer considered to be a dog.

political aspirin

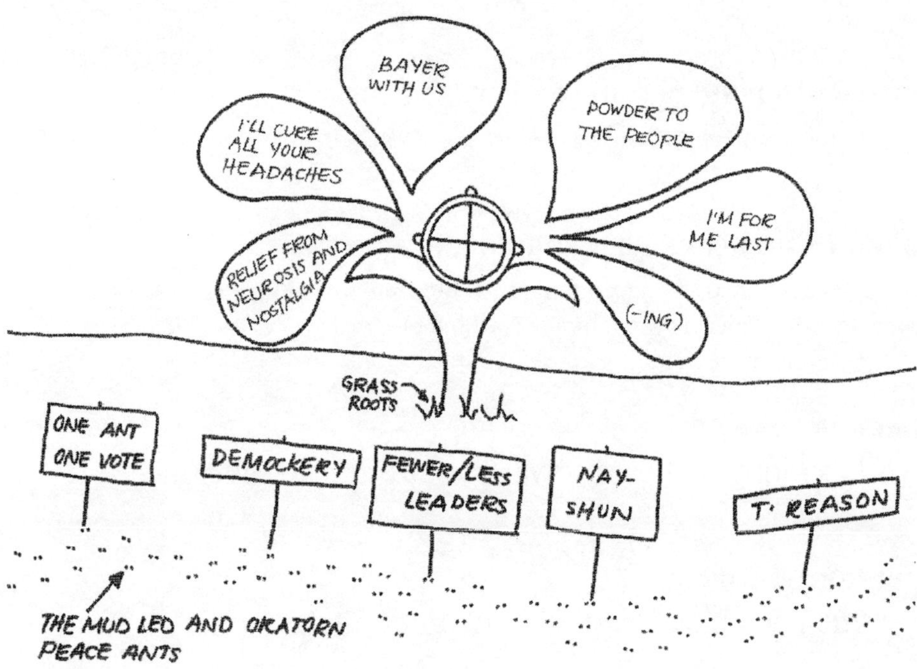

Any resemblance of the aspirin to Jimmy Carter is purely unavoidable.

political correctness backing the side that won

politicians people who go around with their head in the crowds

pornography extracensory perception

postman the era following postmodern after we've killed off ourselves and most macro life
We're too big for our ***boots*** *and too smart for our* ***breaches****!*

postman's holiday Earth taking a long breather after finally conquering this life-threatening disease
posthumus after the final human legacy, our contribution to soil enrichment, is exhausted
posthumorous the present situation and above consequences

preparedness Keep a finger on the panic button at all times.
push the panic button It's something I've often wanted to do but in the excitement I could never find the damned thing.
Which only (im)proves my first argument.

presence of mind A Murphy's outlaw has invaded your head.

pretty pretty somewhat beautiful
Shouldn't a pretty pretty girl be be twice as pretty as a pretty girl?
pretty ugly the average human, a blend of extremes

priority jobs those on your TO DO list the longest

privy the executive toilet
privy counsel legal toilet aid
privy seal
an animal trained to assist with it, like Rabelais' goose wiper
privy chamber pot the object of all the above

out mis
In the US the **Privy Chamber** is called **the ^House of ^Representatives**.

procreation promulgation of the anti-evoution dogma by having lots of kids to inculcate with it

the professional the psychiatrist's couch

We forget psychiatrists started the couch-as-isolation-chamber idea in the first place, culminating in the **vidiocy** of today's potatoes. Give credit where due.

proletariat revolution

when the workers join hands and dance around in a circle

(Because they've just overthrown the square dancing government?)

Revolutions revolve in circles. This is well known **in revolutionary circles**

programmed brainwashed by TV

promised land how politicians since Moses have persuaded people to follow them

pros and cons politicians and scam artists
But I repeat myself, as Mark Twain would say.

Providence "When all else fails, get lucky."

pseudo-intellectual
a thoughtful, erudite person without a degree

psychokinesis when your mind won't stop racing

public opinion what poll writers tell us we believe

quality control Murphy's law
It protects us from a stifling overabundance of quality.

rags to riches "Down with excessive wealth!" "Thieves!" "Capitalist pigs!" "If you're so rich why aren't you smart?" etc

real pecker one who abuses his position in the pecking order

redneck one whose blood stops short of the brain

A Rocky Life

rest on your laurels a good way to puncture your butt

rose-coloured glasses the half full ones

satisfactory a 'no sweat' shop

sausage a mystery food

Till you learn **the offal truth**: may contain ground cow, ground hog, groundhog, ground squirrel, ground beetle, ground ground, ground excretera, exc, exc, exc.

sheep in wolf's clothing armchair war supporters
"It's a sheep eat sheep world!"

shit for brains God's biggest mistake when He created man

smoking heaps of grass
police party disposing of a large marijuana confiscation

spontaneous abortion
quite suddenly deciding to go see that shady doctor

spontaneous generalisation
an outburst of overviews I often suffer from, not unlike
jumping to conclusions:

stuck with the past tense of **stick with** after the enthusiasm dies

Tails you win, heads you lose.
The old story of love.

throwaway society
a brilliant solution to the ecological crisis—throw us *all* away!

stiff upper lip

lipstick

third-degree burns

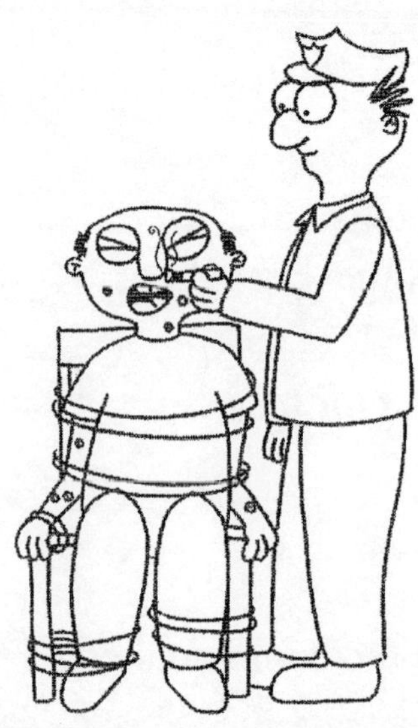

two timers

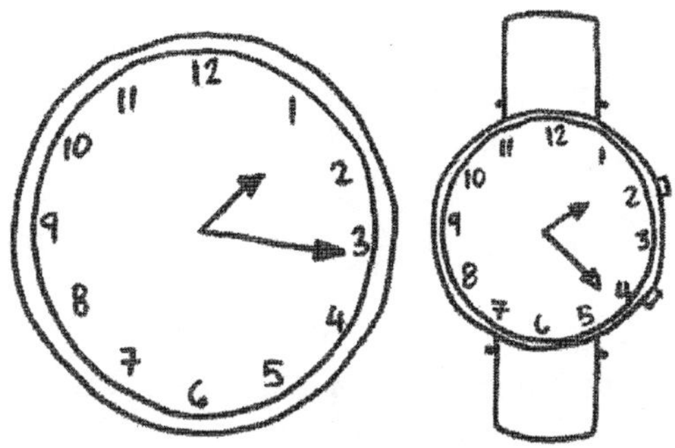

You can't trust two timers to be faithful.

very closed brains a circulatory impairment blocking info inflo; side effect of and often confused with maturity

"**W**" the thick **edge** of the **Wedge**, commonly recognised as the simplest tool

Act II **Bibliofile: Future Tittles 2**

The Nuclear Family as Nuclear Breeder

Here I shall expose the inconvenient truth that the population bomb is a nuclear device, and is threating itself (ie, us). Other members besides arms need control (Don't count on the cytoplasm. It will die off without a breeding nucleus.)

Stasis Symbols and Stranders of Living: The Plight of Symbol Psi Man, Meta-pi Man

This one's a bit hairy and might enjoy a brief expo. A meta-pi man has his head off in other dimensions. Like going to the fair, or seeking status. The only foreseeable cure is to find a gene for status seeking and delete it worldwide. Then we could get on with the job of being the contented cows we're supposed to be.

How We Wound Up Wound Up

Here in a similar vein I advocate letting your watches unwind.
For young readers I should point out that watches used to be spring-driven.

"Medium" Is the Message

This watchword of Mediacracy Mediocracy can be traced to the immoral words of A Pope, *"Be not the first by whom the new is tried, nor yet the last to lay the old aside."* Immoral because, to paraphrase Newton, "If I have seen anything new it is because I have stood on the shoulders of giant fools." Fools are always the first by whom the new is tried, so there's nothing new without them. In contrast, the Medium message is "Don't be a fool! Be medium."

Beyond Nietzsche and Skinner

Here I too stand on the shoulders of giant fools—authors of *Beyond Good and Evil* and *Beyond Freedom and Dignity*—and describe the view from the loft.

Future Shock, Motion Sickness and Enlightenment (Illustrated)

Explains the subtle difference between these three awakening phenomena. Lots of pictures of tasers in action, vomiting passengers, and blissful buddhas.

HOW TO DOUBLE THE MEANING OF LIFE

Act III

SOUNDS ALIKE FUN

INSECTS IN SECTS IN SEX IN SECS

Never eat anything you can't pronounce. — *Erma Bombeck*

Say what you want about the deaf. — *Jimmy Carr*

When I am dead I hope it may be said:
"His sins were scarlet, but his books were read." — *Hilaire Belloc*

cycle path psychopath

The third Act in this Word Play offers pun fun based on sound rather than usage or spelling. It covers three otherwise different forms, as outlined below. They are joined into one act for a phone-y reason because none was substantial enuf to make a separate act. So there, now you know. (The five acts were originally prepared as five books.)

Chapter 6. **SOUND ALIKES** ("Puns")

If I were ever punishèd
For every little pun I shed,
I'd hide me in a punny shed
And there I'd hang my punnish head.
— *Samuel Johnson* (modified Untermeyer version)

Hanging is too good for a man who makes puns.
He should be drawn and quoted. — *Fred Allen / Card Walker*

You can always tell if a lass is Scottish by the way she rolls her Rs.
— *Anon.*

6A. HOMOPHONES AND HOMOPHONIES

These are read-'em-out-loud chapters. This one is another fictionary, the work of an already confessed word phonetic, Ewer Strewly. It poors out puns in the narrow Johnsonian sense (above) of differently spelled sound-alikes or **homophones.** *(No, homophones are not gay hotlines.)* When the homos don't sound exactly alike, they're **homophonies** or Pretenders to the Phone. *(And no, homophonies are not undercover cops in gay bars. Quit asking!)*

Homophon(i)es that are also puns might be called **phonygrams** for the double play on sound and meaning. *(No, you one-track anagrammer! Phonygrams are* *<u>not</u>* **gays morph'n**,*)* Just one version of a homopair is given if the other is obvious. Say obscure ones out loud—or skip them, they won't mind and I'll never know. But if I ever do find out you skipped one, expect a swift, terrifying snub!

adolescence a dull, less-sense, "addle" essence

> *The denunciation of the young is a necessary part of the hygiene of older people, and greatly assists in the circulation of their blood.*
> — *Logan P. Smith*

antique clock wise
learned in retrograde subjects such as old timepieces like Paul Keating

artillery "Hard Hillary–heart Hillary" art Hillary artillery.
Bad cop, good cop at once.

a bad hare day

bills in her ears

battle acts Throwing the frying pan at hubby, for instance.

booze traps Many people try to lift themselves up by these.

carcinogenesis conception
in the back seat (Can it cause cancer??)

cash traitor
the swine who steals my money *and* my purse, and the family jewels in the purse!

cock succour
giving aid and comfort to a bird
(in exchange for fellatio?)

can guru

cigarillo

sick gorilla

daze on end

colonels nuts *(Not nuts! Remember catch-22. — Ed.)*

descent into the abbess missionary position

"Wasn't **dinner great**?"
"Don't dinner-great it! It's a **supper-ate reality**."

divinity inclined to jump into a task totally

domineering expensive earlobe jewelry demanded by overbearing women

eat-up-us complex incestuous cannibalism
"We can't go on eating like this, Mother."

encaged to be married "In this ring I thee web."

ear elephant wears a huge hearing aid and bears no relation to anything

enema a non-friend "With friends like you who needs enemas?"

epic urine drinking only the finest wines to excess

eunuch horn something only dreamed of by unfavoured harem wives and their castrati servants (and by randy horses)

far-in agent 1. a deep cover spy
2. a meditation-enhancing drug or device

foreign white where Western tourists travel and how they're identified

frequent high Freak went "Hi!!" **Off 'n' on?** "Often on!"

~~gnome adder~~ No matter!

This enigmagram for subterraneans (goblins, trolls, etc) got in here by mistake. Forget you saw it and move right along to the next item please. Tell no one. Don't try to decipher it. It has no human meaning, my mole assures me.

Greedings! How bankers say hello to each other.

happy, appetite tight

high pretension
impaired circulation caused by over-seriousness about Art

idolatry a dollar tree
Botanists assure me money *doesn't* grow on trees. *But what do those meddling scientists know? Cut off their branches! Sell them!*

industries In 'dust trees' end us trees.
Justification? "Just a vocation." *(Just defecation!)*

inner fear ants being your own worst vermin

instincts unreleased farts

larkspur a plant that thinks it's a bird that thinks it's a cat

lawyer liar In smart dialects these are pronounced indistinguishably.

liability: the measure of a lawyer —*Anon.*

99% of lawyers give the rest a bad name. — *Steven Wright*

Why experiment with animals when there are so many lawyers about? —*Anon.*

lazy Lay, Z...
US snoring. Contrast...
BRITISH SNORING:

microboat ashore

legislator Leches later. Aha, sexual Congress!

lieutenant one who sleeps in a public toilet — **in loo** of a bedroom

lochness the degree to which one exists in lakes (One *unspotted lizard?*) The lochness scale is used by professional skeptics as an incredibility gauge.

"**No peace,** no piece."
Lysistrata's recipe empowering women to stop wars if they really want to.

officious offish, us, oft vicious

overreaction ovary action Damned female hormones playing up.

Nazi Not see. Why not? They were **blinded by the right**.

patients Patience!
Have you ever been to a doctor and not had to wait? Write me.

waitlessness
This is impossible at the doctor's, it's so *heavy* there.

pedigreed Petty-greed status seekers have their pet "degreed".

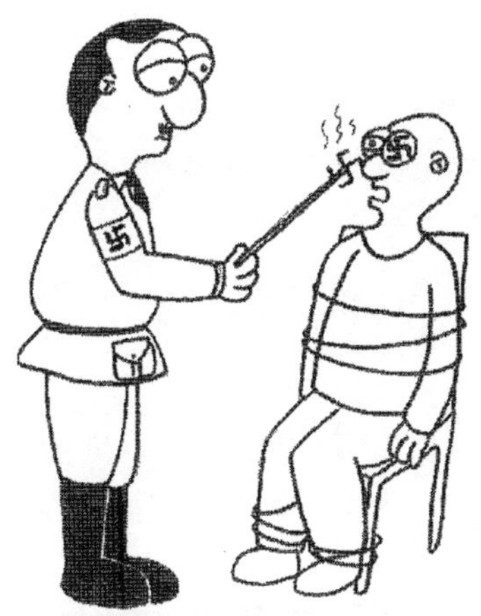

pepper-upper
A wallpaper hanger—he peps up the housewife, especially if he hangs well.

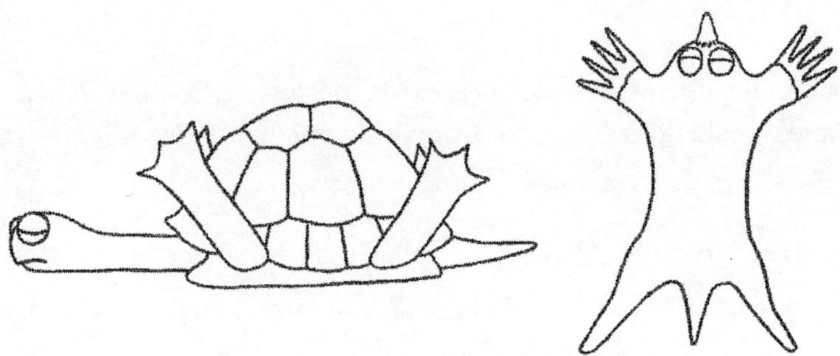

rigor tortoise **rigor a mole**

permutation when a cat's voice cracks at puberty

plaque pretend
dialect, as in "Plaque you've got an achievement award on your wall."

prickly especially
dialect, as in "It's not prickly hot today." or "That's not a prickly prickly pear."

purebred No butter. *(That's "none better"!)*

rechoired Better singers were needed.

reserve wars The backlog of emergency wars to wage if you run out of popular wars; for example, the Bushwhackers were holding Iran, North Korea, Syria and maybe China and Russia in their reserve wars **reservoirs**.

sack-religious worshipping the bed on the Sabbath

sub-bourbon housewife "dropping" out from oppressive conformity

succeed "Suck seed: **succumb,** suck cum."
the Lewinsky formula

tantramatic
a meditation device for calming a tantrum addict

two-thirty time to go to the dentist
Ta to Graeme Bell for this painful pun.

very into resting It's good to sit awhile now and then, I say. You can't lie down all the time. But remember, if you don't get up you can't be put down. *(Hmm,* very interesting*! Just don't let your boss see you reading this.)*

6B. **FEW SAY SO**

A politician is an acrobat: he maintains his balance by saying the opposite of what he does. — *Maurice Barrès*

These sound alikes mean quite the opposite of what they seem. They're to mumble politely when you don't agree with someone. (cf. Feb.'04 *Word Ways.*)

Sounds alike	Actual saying
If you say so.	Few say so.
Sure thing.	'S *your* thing.
Of course.	Off course!
I hear you.	Irer, you!
I dare say.	"I'd airs," eh?
Good reply.	Good? Reap lie.
Depend on it.	Deep end, oh nit.
Rely on it.	Real lyin', it.
Indubitable.	In doo, bit o' bull.
Irrefutable.	Eerie, feudable.
Naturally.	Not, surely!
Plain truth.	*Playin'* truth.
Sensational.	Sense say "Shun all!"
The sky's the limit.	This guy's the limit.

6C. PUNIVERSITY

HEWN-EVER CITY-HEAD-YOU OCCASION

"Hewn-ever..." sounds alike "University Education". Opinions of it vary:

Education: the path from cocky ignorance to miserable uncertainty.
— *Mark Twain*

He that increaseth knowledge increaseth sorrow. — *God*
(Is that why God the Omniscient is so sad, mean and jealous?)

So far as I remember, there is not one word in the Gospels in praise of intelligence. — *Bertrand Russell*

It is not clear that intelligence has any long-term survival value.
— *Stephen Hawking*

Why waste time learning when ignorance is instantaneous?
— *Ray Waterson (Calvin and Hobbes)*

If ignorance is bliss, why aren't more people happy? — *Anon.*

He was sent, as usual, to a public school, where a little learning was painfully beaten into him, and from thence to the university, where it was carefully taken out of him. — *Thomas Love Peacock*

... a storehouse of learning because so little is taken away. — *Anon.*

"That's the reason they're called lessons," the Gryphon remarked [to Alice]: "because they lessen from day to day." — *Lewis Carroll*

Dublin University contains the cream of Ireland: rich and thick.
— *Samuel Beckett*

Education isn't everything. For a start, it isn't an elephant.
— *Spike Milligan*

College is breaking my spirit. Every single day they're telling me things I don't know. It's making me feel stupid. — *The Gilmore Girls*

Refusing to take sides, I proceed with some homophonic puns on a few of the academented Departments here at Puniversity *(Puny Verse at Tea).* The course descriptions are given as clues, and the list is alphabetical by the original name before the department was deconstructed. Mostly from *Word Ways*, Nov. 2008.

Angry Culture
The peasants are revolting.

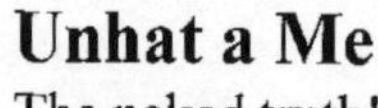

Unhat a Me
The naked truth!

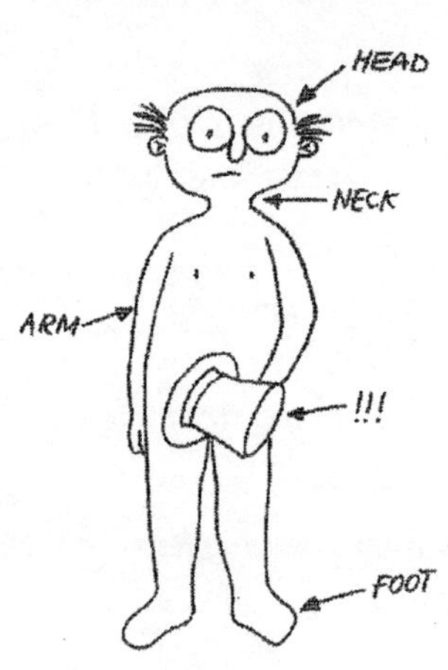

By All a "Gee!"
Study the astonishing, astounding, amazing, remarkably wonderful world of life.

Cow Queue Lust Get in line, learn to <u>differentiate</u> ox tails (*queues,* Fr.) and <u>integrate</u> the appropriate gender into your sex life.

Comp. Pewter Science all the latest high tech materials

> *A computer is like an old testament god, with a lot of rules and no mercy.*
> — *Joseph Campbell*

Drooling and Panting Includes nude model studies!

Eggheads of the world, arise! ... You have nothing to lose but your yolks. — *Adlai Stevenson*

'Head-You' Occasion

Learn, how to get a head in life. Turns rednecks into readheads.

"Etch-You Cage-In!" they reply. "We don't need no thought control!"

I vaguely remember my schooldays. They were what was going on in the background when I was trying to listen to the Beatles. — *Douglas Adams*

TEACHER: *You're late! You should have been here at nine o'clock.*
BOY: *Why? What happened?* — *Anon.*

Inch a Nearing tools at work, zeroing in on precise erections

Ankle Leash Wade deeply into our language, heel to its rules.

Letter Chewer Dig your teeth into its tasty product.

Shakespeare did not write so much in all his life as is written in a single room during one week of examination. Yet some dotards deny progress. — *Walter A. Raleigh* (1923)

Fine Arse

Boys: Enrol in Art School—that's where the prettiest girls are!

Ge ogre, a fee!

Pay up, humanity, before we run out of habitable geography altogether!

Without Geography you would be quite lost. — *W. C. Sellar and R. J. Yeatman, "1066"*

Mad Thematics enough theorems to drive anyone crazy

Meddle Sin

If God wanted us all to be healthy He wouldn't have created disease.

Full awe's a fee. Broad thinking and alert concentration are taxing.

If you're studying Geology which is all facts, as soon as you get out of school you forget it all, but if you study Philosophy you remember just enough to screw you up for the rest of your life. — *Steve Martin*

Poor Tree

Ere it too is chopped away altogether, get thee to the root, flowering and fruits of the quaint old art of versifying, that near extinct cousin of hot novel writing.

In Australia, not reading poetry is the national pastime. — *Phyllis McGinley*

Roam-Ants Slang Wedge Pointed entry into the world of a nomadic **Fringe** group of Mediterranean ants and their colloqualisms. Si, si, includes **Spinach**, the language of Popeye.

So-so-ology All about a mediocre animal that thinks it's God's gift to God.

***The* Ology** Give self-righteousness a schloarly basis.

They "Allah, gee!" Or study the other great Only God.

And on the eighth day God said, "OK, Murphy, you can take over now." — *Michael Redmond*

Worst Turn History Where did it all go wrong?

"So"-ology All the animals that "just are".

6D. SIGNATURE PUNS

They say you shouldn't say nothing about the dead unless you can say something good. He's dead. Good. — *Moms Mabley*

Not many people realise just how well known he is. — *Lord Gowrie*

Any fool can criticise—and many of them do. — *Cyril Garbett*

And here I go. **Signature puns** (anagram: **genius-spun art**!) are sound-alike puns on famous names, mostly biographical 'signatures', some just silly. Most are non-fictional, I've been led to believe. For more see *Word Ways*, Nov. 2006. My model was Kliban's **Mousey Dung** from *Cat*.

Achilles hock kill-ease

Douglas Adams Dug less sad aims.

Harry Belafonte *¡Arriba elefante!*
That's Spanish for topflight giant—or the elephant in the attic.

Lucretia Borgia Lucre-ish hub orgy, huh?
She was the paragon of upper-class depravity, a role model for today's rich.

Salvador Dali self-adored holy **Dali Llama**

Cameron Diaz camera on de ass (an' on de unique smile)

W. C. Fields Double use he fields.

Hippocrates hip pocket rate tease Father of modern medicine!

Dustin Hoffman Does ten "off" men.

J. Hoover "Jehovah"
For decades JEH (aka J. Eager Beaver) was the US God in fancy dress. As his name reveals, he came from a divine egg, **JEHova**. He also founded the J. Hoover's Witnessless Witlessness sect.

L Gecko

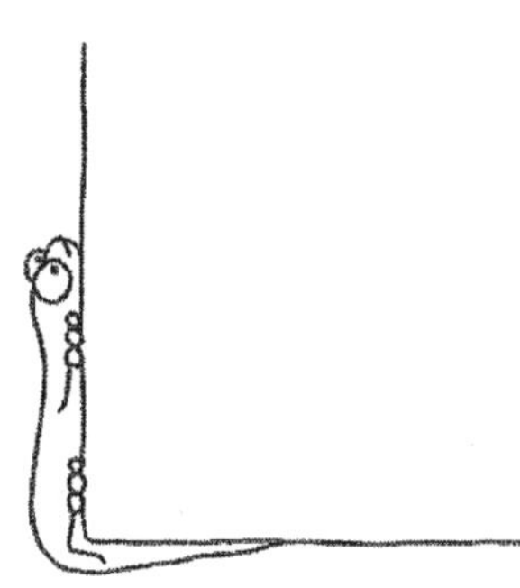

Judas Iscariot
Jew'd assist carry out.
He aided Jesus' plan.

John Keats "junk eats"
Indulgent maybe, but TB got him.

Spike Milligan
"Spy" came ill again.

George Orwell
Jawer? Jawer well!
Did Eric Blair choose this penname for the alliteration?

Louis Pasteur
"Loo is pest tour!"

Rolling Stones raw link's tones

Pete Seeger peace eager

John Philip Sousa "John" fill-ups ooze, huh?
Without his great tunes we wouldn't still have marching bands to put up with.

Guiseppi Verdi "Juice happy," averred he. In Vino Verditas?

Amerigo Vespucci America? Vast pooch! (hee)
A mere ego-vast poo. Sheee!!
Spoiled puppies. *"But it's a puppy-eat-puppy world out there!"*

> *America is a large friendly dog in a small room. Every time it wags its tail, it knocks over a chair.* — *Arnold Toynbee*

Hairy Potter

Donkey Oaty

Chapter 7. **SOUND SWAPS**

May I sew you to your sheet? — *Rev. Wm. Spooner*

The Lord is a shoving leopard. — *ditto*

The waist is a terrible thing to mind. — *Anon.*

He has a man's body on a teenager's head. — *George Graham*

7A. **SPOONERISMS**

Spoonerisms swap the initial sounds of two parts of a word or phrase. Any number of letters. A good example is the anagram **great apes ate grapes**. A majority of those here are also anagrams. A few are what Richard Lederer calls "poonerisms" or sexual spoonerisms, which might also be called forkerisms.

Spoonerisms are named after Reverend Wm. Archibald Spooner (1844-1930), once warden of New College Oxford, who frequently made such boners, eg, **our queer old dean; is the bean dizzy; a nosey little cook; a half-warmed fish; a wining shit; you've tasted two worms**. (Most of these are apochryphal.) He's said to have started as a **bird watcher** but wound up a **word botcher**. See Don Hauptman's fine review of Spoonerisms, *Cruel and Unusual Puns*, Dell, 1991.

Other famous swaps include a radio announcer's **reach for the breast in bed** and the greatest spoonerism ever, Dorothy Parker's

I'd rather have a bottle in front of me than a frontal lobotomy.

Best be the tie that blinds.
Blind faith ties the blind fold.

"Baaa! Hugbum!"
Randy ram, "I wanna be Scrooge!"

bourbon light urban blight

cash transactions
"Trashcans actions!"
Consumerism lashes back.

candle with hare

Congress pro "Progress!" con
Isn't it incongruous that in Congress the pros are cons and the cons are pros'?

Does a diamond dime a dozen?
Pawnbroker's rhetorical negative, like "Does the Pope shit in the woods?"

I'll weigh a fly.

This is a biochemist
preparing to prepare
a tissue of flies.

He heils high heels. a Nazi transvestite

insecticide Insect, aside! (insect aside:)

Knickerbocker bicker knocker
argumentative New York fault-finder; or conversely, one who *knocks* bickering

Lays of Our Dives 1. divers songs
2. adult soap opera set in a sleazy pick-up bar

My socks stink, my stocks sink.
Loveable = a BO level? (anagram)

sex inciting sin exciting
sin sex: ...'s in, 's ex, 's in, 's ex, 's in, 's ex... (a charade)

sucking fun of a bitch fellatio

sunflower fun, slower

sun flōwer

The cursed is wet to yum. *"The worst is yet to come!"*
Oh Hell, I was having such damp fun.

7B. SPOONER'S TRAVELS

War is God's way of teaching Americans geography. — Ambrose Bierce

An "American!" *thinks North America and South America are the two sides in the Civil War and Afro-Eurasia is an LA ghetto. — Name Withheld*

Here are some tourist tips from Rev. Spooner's world travels. The majority are quite insulting, so I apologise on his behalf. He seemed preoccupied with toilet humour as well. From *Word Ways*, August 2009, except that Rev. Spooner's comments (often prophetic) were uncovered later.

Ankara "can" aura §§§
Okay, unfair, I only visited old folks homes.

Athens thin ass (|)
Even a rich Athenian can pass thru the eye of a needle.

Barcelona arsehole boner K
It's not what you think. It's what you do.

Brisbane "biz" brain (toilet biz) (.!.)

Budapest Pooed a best. (It's none of my biz!) (¡)

Buenos Aires Oo, anus berries! ....
more biz residuals

Cayenne "I can!" (Obama's birthplace?) |I|

Hartford fart herd < < < < < < <

What better headquarters for flatulence than the home of a bunch of old insurance farts?

Mexico City sexy committee "_" "_" "_"

Greetings from the street corner.

New Orleans Or new liens!

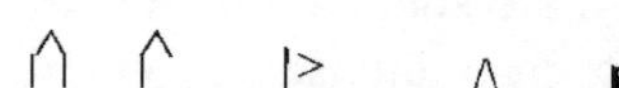

Too sad to be funny. And now new liens fits much of the world.

Panama City Menopause City

Many a US widow retires here.

Paris air piss P

The French are more delicate, pronouncing it **air pee**. And in the wind it can look like the letter P, as in *Urination Unto Yourself.*

Rangoon goon-ran $

Another thug-run military dictatorship (1989-).

San Diego Dancy egg, oh? o/oo o

Its girls are "bopping" to get fertilised.

Timbuktu BM? Took two. (i) (i)

It didn't give *me* the shits. I've never been there.

7C. SIGNATURE SPOONERISMS

The nice thing about being a celebrity is that when you bore people, they think it's their fault. — *Henry Kissinger*

(Not all of us, you BOF.)

...argument as thin as the homeopathic soup made by boiling the shadow of a pigeon — *Abraham Lincoln*

O wad some power the giftie gie us to see oursel's as ithers see us! — *Robert Burns*

Like Signature Puns, these—plus many more in the May 2007 *Word Ways*—are sounds-alike puns on famous names, but instead of direct puns they're puns on Spoonerisms of the names.† I allow latitude in pronunciation for a particularly apt outcome, like in the first up, a self-correcting double spooner honoring the good Reverend himself, whom I had to promote to Bishop posthumously *("well-deserved!")* to get this critter to work. Think alternative time stream. (Truth is, I composed it while mistakenly thinking he *was* a Bishop. Why?)

'Bishop' Spooner Speech hop boner. *(Speech hop booner!)*

Halle Berry belly hairy

What? Is Spooner perhaps confusing her with **"Hairy Belly" Fonda**?

Tony Blair baloney t' air

Tony Blair does the work of two men. Laurel and Hardy. — *Bob Monkhouse*

James Dean "dames" gene

† Brad **Pitt** was oblivious of spoonerisms when naming his child **Shiloh**, poor kid. And don't blame me for calling attention to this unfortunate goof, I saw it in *Word Ways*. Anyway, schoolmates are bound to hit upon it by slip of tongue.

Adam and Eve "Eat 'em and 'ave,"
said the Apple salesman. Naturally, Satan has a lower class accent.

Sigmund Freud "Frig man" saw id.
The frig man saw sex in everything, like the patient who saw sex in every ink blot and blamed the psychiatrist for showing him all the dirty pictures.

Ava Gardner Gave a hardener!

Judy Garland goody-jar land

Germaine Greer "Grr, men!" jeer

Paris Hilton Heiress Piltdown
At first thought to be a pre-human, the specimen has now been revealed to be a scientific hoax concocted by an elaborate media and hi-tech conspiracy.

Thelonious Monk melodious thunk

Elvis Presley pelvis-wrestley

Basil Rathbone Razzle bathbone. A shower lover?

Andy Roddick randy odd hick
"And erotic," says his signature pun.
Whatcha expect with a name like rod-dick?

Jennifer Saunders center for jaundice (*Ab Fab*)

John Philip Sousa song fillip juicer
Does this make up for the rude insult in Signature Puns? I was only joking.
No.
NO? Alright then, I meant every word of it!

John Wayne wan Jane (antonym)

> P.B. *I'm giving John Wayne a book for his birthday.*
> J.F. *He's got a book.* — *Peter Bogdanovich and John Ford*

Malcolm X "All come, mix." (perfect antonym!)

Chapter 8. Poems

A PUN THE WINGS OF SONG

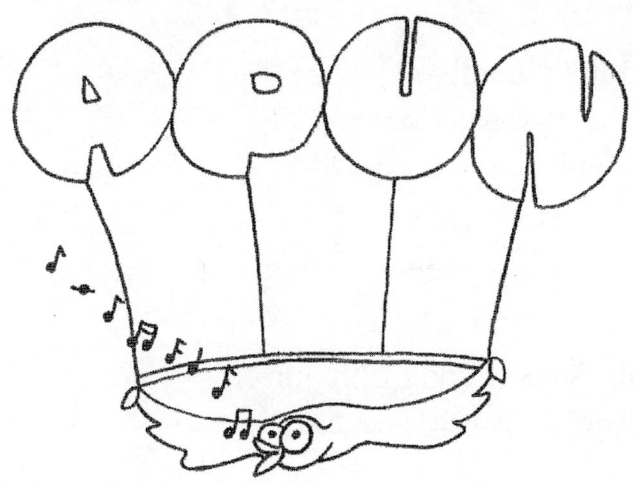

Der spring is sprung, der grass is riz,
I wonder where dem boidies is?
"Der little boids is on der wing." Ain't that absoid,
Der little wings is on der boid! — Anon. (Bronx)

The fellow who is useless at writing poetry still attempts it.
— Horace

One day of the week, if possible, neither read nor write poetry.
— Chinese rule of health

If there's no money in poetry, neither is there poetry in money.
— Robert Graves

A pun can be the springboard, wings and propeller of a song or poem, uncaging the imagination from down-to-earth sobriety and propriety to fly away to exotic lands, deep twists or gay nonsense domains. As you other self-appointed poets out there know, we can get away with most anything if we call it poetry, without fear of the Poetic Justice Dept. Still, I always carry my Poetic License on me.

You may call my opera **suppoetry**. Or if you prefer **sub-poetry**, that's okay, it aims to **subport** you. But if it gives you the shits, just call it **suppose-a-poetry**. (**Bold** marks items involving word or letter play.)

8A. **VERSE, VERSER and VERSED**

CALYPSO DOXOLOGY

Gloria in Excelsis Deo, De-e-e-e-e-e-O.

BATHOLOGY

Vicious killers, tiny slimy darts ——> EAT *the unclean!!* — *Anon.*
(Okay, I made it up.)

We wash before and after
    And run from what is not;
Our sincerest lather
    With some germs is fought;
Our fondest cleans
    Are those that give us sterile brains.

"*HANG LOW*" — THE NATIVE PERSPECTIVE

Anglo, "sweet cheery lot," comin' for to take my home...

THERE'S SAFETY IN NUMBNESS

Money makes the world go funny.
Crime marches on like time.
Liquor makes the world go quicker,
Wine makes the world sublime.

(Way out, man.)

MISCEGENATION IN THE STOCK YARDS (A LOVE SONG)

How now, brown cow
Who knew bruin coo.

Interspecies hanky-panky, or a reference to the aftermath of the "stock" market crash? The cows (bulls) have been "wooed" into the bruins' (bears') camp. **Wow, woe, woo**, in that order. (Coo, meaning woo, is also slang for wow.)

OPEN DECK TO ME

Literary critics sat on their buttix
Eating our hearts as they fried us.
We're the creators, they're just master baiters.
Why then let *their* **pen decide us**?

Critic's reply: *"This guy's in need of a 'pen dick's' operation hisself!"*

The little glow-worm sits and glows,
As brilliant as the stars,
But you'd be wrong if you suppose
That he will light cigars. — *A. P. Herbert*

JUST ONE LITTLE CANDLE

If everyone lit just one little candle,
And on the next night two,
And on the next night four,
And so on for three or four months,
The earth would be brighter than the sun
And an ocean of tallow engulfing the moon.
(So forget it, hey?)

HORMONE DERANGE (screwed up, an old song)

Whore-hormone derange
Where the deer and the ant elope, play,
Where cell-dumb is herd, a disco raging weird,
And these guys air "knot cow" deeds all day.

MISTAKEN IDENTITIES

THE CHICKEN WHO WASN'T
Why did the chicken cross the road?
'Cause it *wasn't chicken!* Like a toad.

THE DUCK WHO DIDN'T
Why did the duck not cross the road?
'Cause it *didn't duck!* End of ode.

Moral: don't count your chickens before they cross the road.

CEMENTALITY A CONCRETE POEM

I know what I must and seek no more,
I have quit moving,
I have *become* the old road,
In it, no longer *on* it,
Stuck behind in deep hardness.

INTIMATIONS OF MORTALITY

Lives	(hums)
.loves	.(humbles)
..laughs	..(humours)
...leaves	...(humus).

NULLARBOR LULLABY

in ForG

On the day to the kangaroo we sipt on a peel
which circumwent the toadstool without apparent if
either in the running and in eating at the bandicoot
which viewed under starfish is almost always usual
thru Nullarbor wallaby's cowallaby heir
leaping to'ad:[ ]:hallucinations:[ ]:foregut saying preyers
in time for rivet time for rivet alone all newts
come out at toadfrog whenever earth eclipse
sheerwise owlwise otherwise pussydog
toadfrog counter log counter tax toad facts
frog file double file nail claws scape cause
toad clause frog paws leep frog mounting creek
anuran spring peppered string slimy love skin touch
amplex tape voice nonscrew rivet pouch
if we toadfrog soon enough toadfrog more-
over and overwrought underwrite toadfrog
arrow poison frog rhythms bowed bow wow now
jazz gigs frogstool cat's pianorana blends
bulltoad drumstick bass bass founder place
craving the toadfrog down to the trogbone
toadfrog left bog whole log shagooon
'gooon toadpole go on happening
go on frogging toard toadfrog Happening
tail gone tale told tailless gate eggs mate
eggs cleave legs fried tongue-tied toad-toed
toad frog gorf daot golf flog toadfrog
togadorf toke fraud food trag toadfrog
frog tag towed toad frog frag toadfrog
tadfrog frogfrog frogtoad toadfrog
frogtoad goadtoad forgatod toadfrog
forgatod forgadot forgadot forgadet
forgedet forgetet forgetit; forget it.
toadfrog toafdrog tofardog tforaodg
ftrooagd frtoogad frotgoad frogtoad
frogtoadfrogtoadfrogtoadfrogtoadfrog
toadfrogtoadfrogtoadfrogtoadfrog

toadfrog toadfrog toadfrog toadfrog
toadfrog toadfrog toadfrog toadfrog
toad frog toad frog toad frog toad frog
toad frog toad frog toad frog toad frog
toad   frog   toad   frog   toad   frog   toad   frog
toad   frog   toad   frog   toad   frog   toad   frog
toad   frog   toad   frog   toad   frog   toad   frog
toad frog toad frog toad frog toad frog
toad frog toad frog toad frog toad frog
toadfrog toadfrog toadfrog toadfrog
toadfrog toadfrog toadfrog toadfrog
toadfrogtoadfrogtoadfrogtoadfrog
toadfrogoadfrogoadfrogoadfrog
toadfrdgadfrdgadfrdgadfrog
toadftogdftogdftogdfrog
toadfoagfoagfoagfrog
toa[illegible]rog
to[illegible]og
t[illegible]g
toadfrog
toadrog
tofdog
tdadg
fuag
[illegible]
[illegible]
[illegible]
[illegible]
[illegible]
[illegible]
[illegible]
[illegible]
[illegible]
[illegible]
z
ż
z
z
z
z
saw log
toadfrog

A.

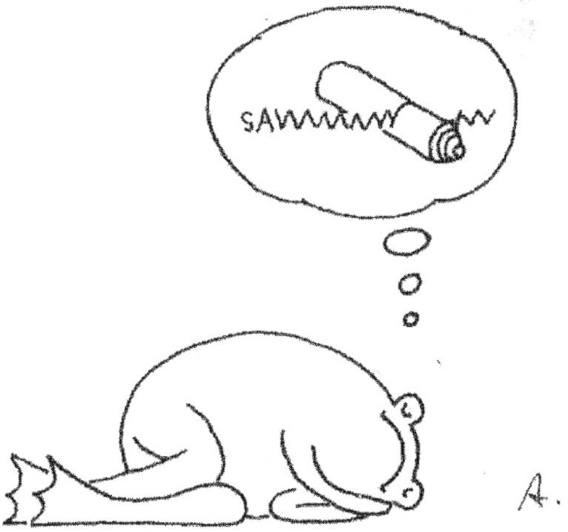

8B. NURSERY CRIMES

Little Miss Muffet sat on her tuffet,
So nobody could get at it.
Along came a spider
And sat down beside her—
But he couldn't get at it either.
— Anon.

Little Bo Peep has lost her sheep
And thinks they may be roaming.
They haven't fled;
They've all dropped dead
From nerve gas in Wyoming.
— Frank Jacobs, Mad, 1972

1.
Jack and Jill went "up the hill"
To share a little liquid.
Jack's fell down and brought a frown
And Jill said "What a dickwilt!"

2.
Little Miss Portion
Sat on a fortune,
Eating her insides, and hey—
Along came a shyster
And smartly advised her
And lightened her fortune away.

Pity this next poor soul as well:

3.
Little Bo Peep
Has gone to sleep
And doesn't know she's in trouble.
With nary a bleat
From her lost sheep
Her retirement plan's in rubble.

I told her not to invest in livestock! "Will come home" indeed.

4. Mary Mary quite contrary,
Why are you down on it all?
Nor silver bells nor cockle shells
Give you a cheering call.

Mary Mary extraordinary,
Why won't your garden glow?
'Cause bells and shells like pretty belles
Won't grow if you doubt them so.

5. Mary had a little lamb, plus nine and ninety others.
The latter didn't go astray, they bonded tight like brothers.
When the stray one went to school
They stayed back in a huff rage.
"Oh *Unfairness* of it all: damn punk gets all the coverage!"

Why do 99 people out of 100 identify with the 1 sheep in 100 that went astray?

6. Mary had a litttle lamb
With mint and applesauce,
But choked on it wondering,
"Is this one Bo Peep lost?"

7. Mary had a little lamb
She named what she shouldna oughter,
And everywhere that Jesus went,
Mary cleaned up after.
Down at the abbatoir one day
She learned of Jesus' slaughter.
It made poor Mary weep and moan
But caused lamb-eaters laughter.

8. SMASHING PUMPKINS

Peter Peter, pumpkin eater,
Had a wife and couldn't beat her.
Put her on a pedestal,
There he kept her till she fell
From the height and cracked her shell.

For she eventually dozed off and fell down and broke her crown and Peter Peter came running after it was too late. They charged him with third degree person-slaughter. Moral: Let your wife come down from her pedestal now and then.

NOTE ADDED IN PRESS:
They later pinned another nursery crime on Peter Peter on the same charge, shell breaking. Guess which one? Hint: it's a famous omelette recipe.

9. JACKS OFF AND RUNNING

Little Jack Horny
Sat with his porny,
Eating his birthday suit.
Jack be careful,
Jack be quick,
Or Mama won't think you're so cute!

10. C.I.A. BLUE

Little Boy Blue come blow your cover.
"Jihad's in the closet! The Reds still hover!"
No, Little Blue, put fear out to pasture,
Else what's a meadow for, I ask yer?

11. CAT

As I was going to St. Ives
I met a cat with seven lives,
And every life had seven charms,
And every charm had seven costs,
And every cost had seven hidden costs,
And every hidden cost had seven more deeply hidden costs...
(At this point I sensed that this might go on indefinitely and moved on.)

Question: How many cat's were going to St. Ives? Answer below. It's a trick question so pause here if you want to think about it first.

Answer: Just the one, me(ow!). That other charmed cat wasn't going anywhere, by the weigh, it was too burdened down with sevenings. And as if that weren't enough, it was two lives short of the customary nine, poor thing.

12. OVER THE MOON

Hey diddle diddle,
The cat got my tongue...

Sorry about that. I believe but can't prove that it was that charming St. Ives cat that dislinguished me. In the end I was dissuaded from going to St. Ives as it's a dangerous place to be without a tongue.

13. THE LOAFER

There was an old woman who lived in a shoe.
She saw off her children and didn't know what to do,
So she took a pension and moved into a more comfy shoe to
Retire and do nothing. The end.

(Shoe off, paparazzi, let her enjoy it! She's no longer a celebrity.)

14.

FOZZY WOZZY

Fozzy Wozzy was a bear,
Fozzy Wozzy had no care...
—Till the Loggy Woggies came!
Now Fozzy Wozzy
Doesn't have a fozzy, dozzy?

Fozzy is Oz-like slang for forest. A coinage I'm told, but I thought I'd heard it.

CAN'T SEE THE FOZZY FOR THE TREES...

...HAVE ALL BEEN LOGGED.

15. NURSERY RHYMES

Cursory
Nursery
Bursary
Anniversary:
Mother Goosery!

2028 will mark the 400th birthday of Mother Goose, Charles Perrault. If you feel that "Goosery" doesn't rhyme with Nursery that would be because he wrote fairy tales, not nursery rhymes. As consolation and in commemoration I throw in a Fairy Tale Crime next, introduced by a 3-4-10 haiku.

16. SOWHAT

Sticks and stones
May break my bones...
Or I can use them to build a house with.

17. STICKS AND STONES

Three little pigs
Tripping on Nature...
Big Bad Wolf came around in a huff
To their house of grass and had a puff...
And they all got stoned.

(But people who live in grass houses shouldn't come to the attention of the Big Bad Pig.)

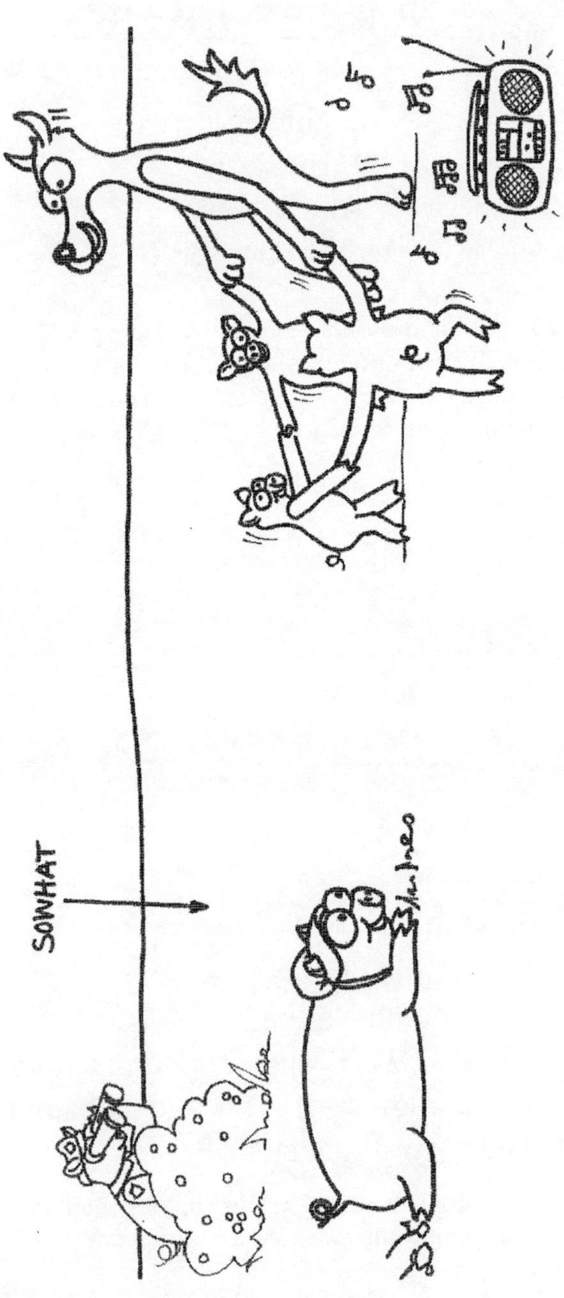
SOWHAT

8C. **MINIMALIST POEMS**

(TRIODES, PENTODES, etc)

GIST OF A WEDDING

Aisle, Altar, Hymn. — *Benny Hill*

Triodes, such as the above classic, are 3-legged critters that manage like a tripod to stand alone on their three metrical feet. Similarly **pentodes** are 5-word pent up odes, while many anagrams in Act IV are **diodes**.

\ DI 'OADS /

Coincidentally, most of the pentodes and **hexodes** presented here happen to be word ladders: each word differs from the next by one letter.

<u>ON HONOUR, HONEST!</u>

A man enters law—to get <u>On</u>.
He remains there—to get <u>Oner</u>.
He retires from the law—to get <u>Onest</u>. — *Anon.*

PSEUDOCOMPARATIVES,
like the above beauty and the **triodes** on the rest of this page, add -er and -est sounds where they don't belong, recalling the title of 8A, "**Verse, Verser** and **Versed**."

<u>COMPARATIVELY RISKY</u>

Mole molar molest?

Who would dare be a pain in the tooth to an underground figure?

<u>COMPARATIVELY UNADORNED</u>

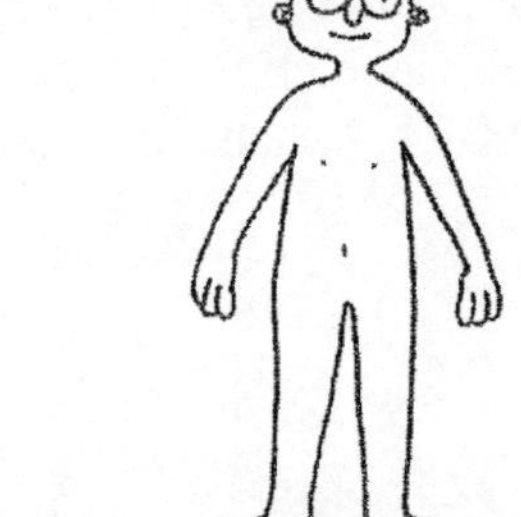

nude neuter nudist

<u>COMPARATIVELY DISGRUNTLED</u>

sow **sour** **soused**

HOW TO FRENCH KISS

Lick her liquor licker.

SUPPORT GROUP FOR A "CHALLENGED" TYPE

Synonymous Economists Anonymous — all at **SEA**

2008 saw its ranks swell hugely with humiliated think-alike financial "gurus".

ILL, VAIN VILLAIN $[V^{ILL}{}_{AIN}]$

Preys, prays praise.

OWNEROUSNESS

Possessions possess possessor. In other words it's a case of **possession possession possession** —things one *"had to have"*.

FRACTAL POLES : GREEN v. BROWN

in seed inspire instinct | exceed, expire, extinct.

FLEA LIB

The ~~drop-out~~ jump-out tale of an eleutheromaniac flea. It...

flees fleas' fleet's fleece.

SKELETAL HUMOUR

THE CHANT OF A STAND-UP SKELETON

FUNNY

BUNNY BONNY

BONEY BONES

For a giggle say it out loud, repeatedly. Funny bunny bonny boney bones. It's musical, tickling the funny bones. It was the highlight of that bonehead's act.

HOME TRUTH

In best

incest, invest

"in-nest" in zest!

LOVE AT FIRST NIGHT

Dating, Eating, Rating, Sating, Mating.

The first verse here is not a pentode but serves to introduce the one that follows, a vowel cascade.

ROCK WITHOUT ROLL

A rolling stone gathers no moss
In its brief sojourn downhill,
But then the bottom ends its toss
And it's free to gather moss at will!

Mass

mess miss

moss, muss.

The mass mess is Civilisation, which *like a rolling stone* is too preoccupied with rolling Nature to have time for mussy things like gathering flowers and moss. It's both a moss misser and a moss musser.

ANOTHER PRISONER OF THE SYSTEM

Hound,

found bound,

wound sound

'round pound:

"Get me outa this dammed **kennel —*'kin'ell!"*** howled the innocent dog.

THE FLOWERING OF HISTORY

or Revolutions Revolve in Circles

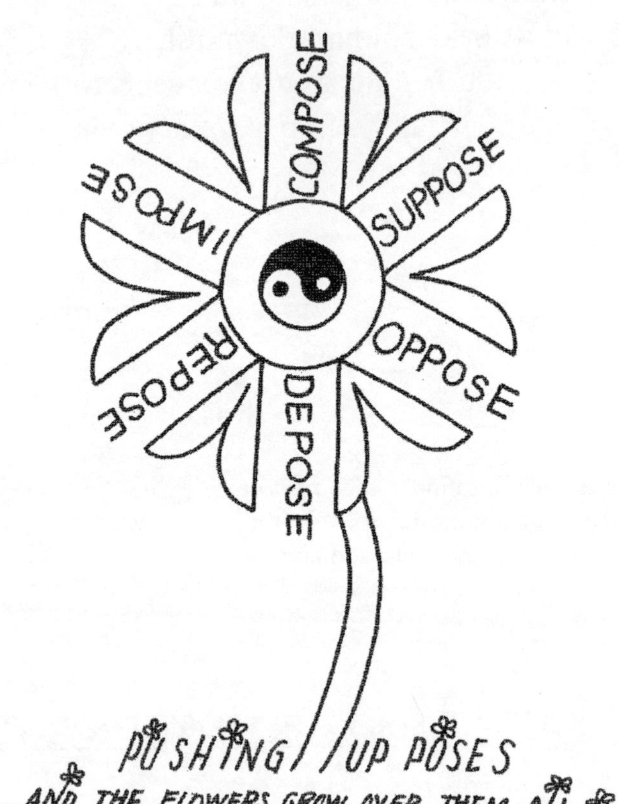

OZONE HOLINESS

UV us up? Ug! *Un-uh!!*

IN BOVINE CIRCLES

COW

COO **LOW**

POO **MOW**

MOO

Read clockwise from the top, **...cow, low, mow, moo, poo, coo, cow...,** this is the life cycle of the low-ly cow. Mow = graze, coo = mate, the final cow = calve then repeats as cow. The following drawn poem, **Grass Roots**, gives the other side of the same coin. The above hexode (heptode counting cow twice) is a shortcut version of roughly the same story but you don't have to die.

GRASS ROOTS:
grass belongs to every one.
until it's eaten
and milked. and spanked. and raised. to love grass.
and rooted. and buried.
and over grown with grass.

8D. **POLYANAGRAM VERSE**

[Writing poetry] starts as inspiration and ends as a crossword puzzle.
— *John Betjeman*

Anagram poetry is just the opposite. It starts as a crossword puzzle and with luck and/or persistence ends as inspiration. Judge for yourself in this punnish selection of light to heavy anagram critters mostly from *up/dn* where I argue that the anagram is an art form and a tool for creative expression.

Polyanagrams are seamless strings of two or more anagrams of one **bold** target or headword(s). The headwords generally serve as the poem titles, but some have titles (and comments) in a different typeface which are not anagrams.

"Historically"
AN EPIC POEM

Lithic royals,
Chariot silly,
O, this racy ill!
Thy liars† coil
Oratic shilly.
"Chaosy!" I trill.

---

† cit.: Holy Liars, **historic events' winners**, invent "news", rich stories. Oratic shilly [shally] means rewording history to suit the victors.

Legislator

Ill tsar-ego, Arts "illego",
Gores a till, a ogre still.
Orgies t' all, Gits o'erall!

CALLS HOME, "SHALL COME"

Sad melancholy ET
–and Halley's comet–
Call home, end stay,
And yet shall come.

Silicone Valley
or Valley of the Dollops

In Cloy Vale lies a veil.
Closely in live a
silly cone clone.
"As lively I live, cone I sally.
Cone is evil ally."

Cleavage = a gel cave?

Outstanding Astounding-Tasting DONUT!

Sing and tout gin and stout,
Donatin' guts and in t' gout.
Giant donuts → donut giants!

Plus an ***outstanding*** bill for the donuts.
(Dedicated to Homer Simpson.)

Human Doings
a poem without rhyme or reason

Om handing us,
Hams undoing,
Moaning "duhs"
As dim hung on,
Dug in on sham.

Conformity

Fit coy norm
On city form.
"In for My cot!"
In comfy rot.

A LOVE POEM

Gay Duo Guy Ado:
"O, gaudy!"
"You dag!"

A HIPPEE HYMN

FOUND IN AN EMPTY BOTTLE OF BEER
FLOATING IN THE OCEAN OF CONSCIOUSNESS

Beer? Weed?

Beer → wee'd.
Weed → Be-er.

∴ Be weeder,
be weeerd,
breed "Wee!"

WORD PLAY

REVEALING ALL THE SECRETS OF THIS OCCULT PRACTICE

Plod awry, wordy pal.
Drop y' law-wary plod.
Warp oldy polyward.
Draw ploy rawly, doppl'r-do way.

Doppeler (bastardised German) is a doubler of meanings,
so 'doppeler-do' is double do-ings, dodo.

8E. **POETIC LICENTIOUSNESS**

Tear out this section if you can't keep it away from children or if you object to the way children are made. It's so lewd that even my Poetic License may not protect me from the Poetic Justice Dept.

QUICK TRICK

an icky poem

Slick prick,
Brick-thick hick-crick chick
click,
sick-lick,
tick-quick stick prick,
dick-flick Watson-Crick.

Watson-Crick is the thinking man's term for DNA, ie, sperm.

WEDDING NIGHT

a polyanagram

NUPTIALS, ...

Pulsatin', I plant "Us", pin a lust.
A unsplit-laps unit, alit,
Spun tail puns:
"Up, Stalin!", "until sap!" an' "tu-lips!"

Wedding night, groin-joined, making dirty jokes
about his "dicktator", her "two lips" and a pun on "sap".

NEW FANGLED BLUES

Another woman done took my woman,
 Liberated her from me.
New-fangled blues is all I got now.
 I'm jest as blue as pink can be.

Went to my old dog Blue for solace.
 (Man's best friend is a sure-fire fuck.)
But Blue was gone and I was bluer:
 Son of a bitch ran away with the duck.†

Ran to my Mamma's womb to hide in:
 Some big mother fucker was already there.
Mom said, "Son, I won't be a minute,
 Then I'll love you—if you cut off your hair!"

In desperation I turned to the Devil,
 Offered my soul in exchange for his love.
He said, "My ancient offer is off now:
 I've just made peace with my Old Man above."

I climbed a tree naked to court its affection.
 It severed a branch and I fell on my ass.
As a final resort I turned my love inward,
 But yanked my root out—and was cured at last!

---

† Daughter of a bitch ran away with the drake, to get technical. This poem was originally published in the Uni of Western Australia student guild *Bullet* in 1974.

BIBLIOFILE III. Future Tittles 3

My daughter thinks I'm nosy. At least that's what she says in her diary. — *Sally Poplin*

Cockroach Orange, a Cook Book

Turn a problem into a delicacy. Other practical recipes: mice-in-a-blanket, roast ratso, horsefly pudding, spotted dick, and that perennial favourite, blackbird pie.

Man Overbored: Another Uninteresting Biography

Ironically a very interesting volume, it turns out. It uniquely probes the absolute depths of plainness, paradoxically achieving startlingly new heights of ennui. Outstandingly boring enough that I hope to sell it to reality TV.

Al Capone, Superscar

A libretto based on epic scrapes between Scarface and the Mighty Ness Monster. Featuring the all-virgin chorus, The Untouchables. Not to be confused with...
The Lonely Ness Monster, that hidden beast we all encounter at times.

Oneness in Tunis

A howdunit mystery in which an Arab couple achieve mutual transcendental consciousness through Tantra and are tried for heresy. Guess whether they care.

Neurology, a Nerve Ending Story

Popular science at its most nerve-tingling, nail-biting, raw-edge best. Your kids will sit up in stunned, bemused fascination as you read it to them.
(This precis was written by the self-deluded narcissistic author. In fact the book looks to be so boring it will make perfect bedtime reading. Highly recommended for that purpose. — Ed.)

Axolotl Questions, Quetzalcoatl Answers

A narrative poem in Q&A format. The Mexican albino salamander asks of the Aztec God answers to deep questions like "When will I grow up?" But sadly it remains a tadpole all its life and never grows up. It's been a role model for me and one or two other men, including this next dude.

THE ADVENTURES OF SUB-DUDE

There will be eight tittles in this semi-magnificent saga.

I. Being Vain in Vain

The best laid plans of Sub-Dude oft go astray.

II. Rebel Without Effect

Sub-Dude has a fruitless go at disestablishmentarianism.

III. Waking Up from the American Dream, or A Walk Through the Valley of the Shadow of Debt,

Sub-Dude flirts with antidisestablishmentarianism, finding temporary direction in rampant consumerism, until the unmuzzled jaws of the free market bite again, as ever. "Free market, my arse," Sub complains. "It cost me everything!"

IV. Whatsupmanship, or A Walk Through the Valley of the Shadow of Doubt,

Penniless and aimless, Sub-Dude wallows in confusion and self-pity.

V. Lost in the Bewilderness, or Where Are You Atman?

Every time Sub thinks he's found himself, he loses track of where it is.

VI. Hanging Out with the Hernia Crowd

In blundering through life Sub-Dude experiments with taking the "hang loose" and "drop out" ideals to the logical extreme. Read all about this disastrous turn.

VII. I Lost My Marbles in the Glass Bead Game

Sub looks for meaning in every direction, orthodox and unorthodox, and it drives him round the bend.

VIII. Transcendental Lobotomy, or Who Needs Brains If They Only Get You Into Strife?

Sub finally achieves peace of (no) mind and finds his true place as one of the unthinking sheep. And lives happenlessly ever after. Well, he'll die some day of course. And be forgot, but for this chronicle. Which will itself be forgot. Amen.

Act IV

LETTER RIP

GREAT APES ATE GRAPES

APPLES WEREN'T OUR UNDOING BUT A FALL FROM GRAPES

ACT IV CONTENTS

THANKS AGAIN

Thanks again to all those cited in the beginning, especially Sue Melton, Robert McGough, and those associated with *Word Ways* (Ross Eckler, Jeremiah Farrell, David Morice, Howard Bergerson and Martin Gardner). Much of this Act and scattered items in other Acts (except the first) were previously published in *Word Ways: the Journal of Recreational Linguistics* from 2001 onwards or in my Word Ways monograph #5, *up/dn, a Dictionary and Contradictionary of Anagrams and Pals* (2002; $10). The journal and monograph are available from the editor, Jeremiah Farrell, 9144 Aintree Drive, Indianapolis IN 46250 USA, or via the Word Ways website: wordways@butler.edu.

Brainy Animals of the HIPPOCAMPUS

LETTER RIP

Baron Frankenstein was a lonely man until
he learned how to make friends. — *Anon.*

In this, the fourth Act of *How to Double the Meaning of Life*, I take word play to violent extremes—tearing words apart. But it's followed by fondling and resetting the letters in the funniest or most apt way discoverable. Anagrams and palindromes are familiar examples, to which I add other types of character abuse including changing letters. On the softer side I include a logology trick called "charades" in which the letters aren't shuffled at all, just respaced or repunctuated. I call them static anagrams. Sub-chapters cover different types of letter and punctuation play, but the critters all wind up as the usual willy-'nilly mix of daffynitions, gags and satire. Titles if any and remarks in a different typeface are not part of the letter play.

Chapter 9. **ALPHABET SOUFFLÉ**
(Anagrams)

A well-crafted anagram is a miniature work of art.
— *David Morice*

Thy genius calls thee not to purchase fame
In keen iambics, but mild anagram:
Leave writing plays, and choose for thy command
Some peaceful province in Acrostic Land
Where thou mayest wings display and altars raise
And torture one poor word ten thousand ways. — *John Dryden*

The Bible is like a person, and if you torture it long enough, you can get it to say almost anything you'd like it to say.
— *Episcopal Rev. Dr. Francis H. Wade*, quoted in *Funny Times*

A cucumber should be well sliced, and dressed with pepper and vinegar, and then thrown out, as good for nothing. — *Samuel Johnson*

Anagrams resemble the Bible. If not Divinely inspired at least capable of saying most anything you like. Whether they resemble sliced cucumbers is your call, but the Johnson quote describes anagramming to a tea if you change "out" to "about" and "nothing" to "something else". It starts with a letter shuffle-scuffle, like a food fight with sliced cucumbers, upseting the natural order of things. But a broken egg can be turned into a soufflé. Just mix and bake to taste. The result may be delicious or tasteless depending on your taste or lack thereof. Anagrams often say apt things I would never have thought of, and some I'd dare not say without the excuse "The letters made me do it!"

The targets are **bold**, their anagrams are fine, although you may disagree with the latter claim. Comments are not part of the anagramming.

I often join two or more anagrams of a target seamlessly into a **polyanagram**, a coherent statement about the target. It's like baking a large soufflé in more than one pan and joining up later. For example, six anagrams of **presentation** can be linked up to form a polyanagram description of a

snore patient: Note net aspir|ant's ripe tone| "nose patter" in| noise pattern| presentation| in prone state.

9A. **GREAT APES ATE GRAPES**
A BRIEF FICTIONARY OF ANAGRAMS

WILLIE: *This is a jigsaw.*
ALF: *It's broken!*
WILLIE: *That's the object. You have to put it together.*
ALF: *Why? I didn't break it!* — *ALF*

I just spent two weeks doing a 100-piece jigsaw. I was quite pleased with myself because on the box it said 6-8 years. — *Les Blake*

All Americans a race in malls

analysis Anil says.

anatomy to many a man a toy

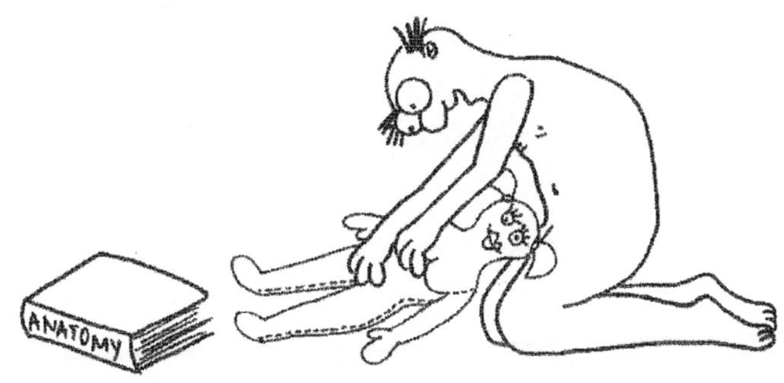

before time Of bit ere me. *My* theory of The Beginning of Time.

burping up-bring [B^{U}R^{P}ING]
(No! Burping shows poor *upbringing.)*

Cafeterias Eat “fare” (sic). (a sic joke)
Cite fear as I cast free a care—ie, fast!

charitable a real bitch (antonym—or a description of Angelina Jolie?)

“Cleanliness ’tis next to Godliness.”
Nice lens: Godliness is next to last.
Apologies to cleaners whose livelihoods may be threatened by this dirty joke.

Hygiene is the corruption of medicine by morality. — H.L. Mencken

cock and bull story lusty candor-block

constipation panic in toots in I-can’t-poots,
‘**motionless**’ stem in loos in me stools (toots = loos = toilets)

couch potatoes pouches to a cot (Such too ace pot?)
Too much pot produces **passive smokers**.

Councillors (two views) 1. Lo, nil occurs. 2. No, *ill* occurs!

destination station I end at (so I intend!)

dining Dig Inn 'n' dig in!

copulation explosion O sex pollution, o panic!

You love and propagate—and ya go overpopulate!

Extra population → → → extrapolation up.

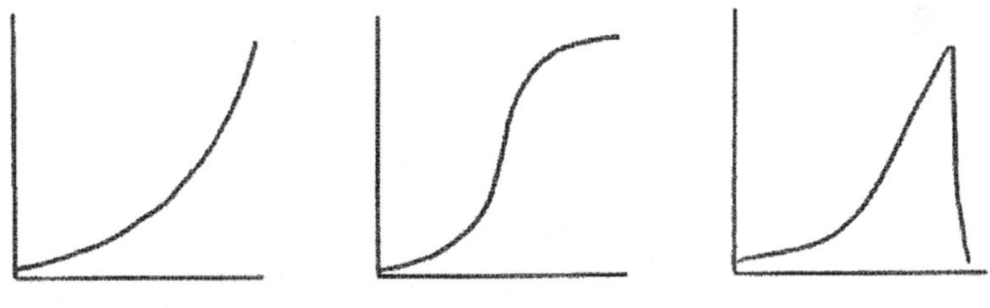

CAPITALIST THEORY BIOLOGICAL THEORY ECOLOGICAL THEORY

OUR REWARD FOR BEING CROWDED IS IT FORCES US TO BE CLEVER, ENOUGH TO BECOME MORE CROWDED. WE CALL IT PROGRESS.

WITHOUT OUR TECHNOLOGY WE WOULDN'T BE ABLE TO PUT THRU THE PROGRAMS REQUIRED TO CREATE THE TECHNOLOGY REQUIRED TO PUT THROUGH OUR PROGRAMS.

THE CORSAIR PIRATE AND HIS COARSE AIR PARROT

(a foreshortened story)

Corsair pet: "Pirates, cor!" ices parrot, "Tropic arse crap site! Or ripe scrota!"

Corsair pet lot: Parrot ice lost.

PEG LEG PETE, RUM RUNNER, & CORSAIR PET

Clop clop.

Who's there?

Some crippled bloke with a dead parrot. Says he's a famous smuggler.

Cow reasoning, sow ignorance.

Formula for dumbing down the populace by intimidation and ridicule of free thought.

cow reasoning **sow ignorance**

doghouse good hues, huge doos

This is an antonym. Dogs don't do their own interiors.

domesticated animal Man! "At domicile" sated as it tamed man docile, **a henpecked ethic**, "the chickened ape".

Editor "Redo it!" Someone else is in the doghouse now. *(You, Anil! Ed.)*

ejaculates a jet clause

"I'm coming!!" Tom ejaculated. — *Anon.* The very first Tom Swiftie?

Embryologic "Come boy/girl by coil o' germ."
(Embryo Logic = by Rome logic.)

Embryo logic is the same as Roman logic: "TO MULTIPLY, DIVIDE!"

"elite snot" nose title
(Lord Nose, you onerous oldy!)

LORD NOSE

Esoteric Sex A handbook of...
exotic Seer's
erotic sexes'
exercises to
excite eros's
sexiest core.

fast food fat foods
(food afts? off toads? staff doo?)
Afts = leftovers (Do they call it "fast" food because it has no nutritional value?)

fearlessness *Far less sense!*

flatteries fatter lies $[^{F}{}_{L}{}^{ATTER}{}_{IES}]$
"explained" expand lie $[^{EXP}{}_{L}{}^{A}{}_{I}{}^{N}{}_{E}{}^{D}]$

foibles self bio!

foreplay fly opera

fornicates can-fit eros (Can't if sore. Sore if can't.)

CONFESSIONS OF AN ANOREXIC

"**Fashionable**, I flash a bone—ie, has no flab.
"**Dietings?** I'd ingest dingiest stingied indigest.
"**A diet acme?** Emaciated!
"**Enviable thin-ism?** The invisible man."

BY POPULAR DEMAND, DR. DUCK'S FAMOUS **ANOREXIA PILLS**

future shock "Fuck, sure hot!"  Goodbye, cool world.

Get it together. "Get her to get it."
(**Gets a lot**? Got least!)

gluttonousness on tongue's lusts, **gluttonous** 'loo-stun' gut

greed de-reg.

One of man's oldest exercises in moral philosophy is the search for a superior moral justification for selfishness. — John Kenneth Galbraith

harrowing hair wrong
A very bad hair day indeed—it's standing on end!

hermaphrodites
part his/her mode,
or mid-part he/she
(Dorm rap: "She-he-it!")

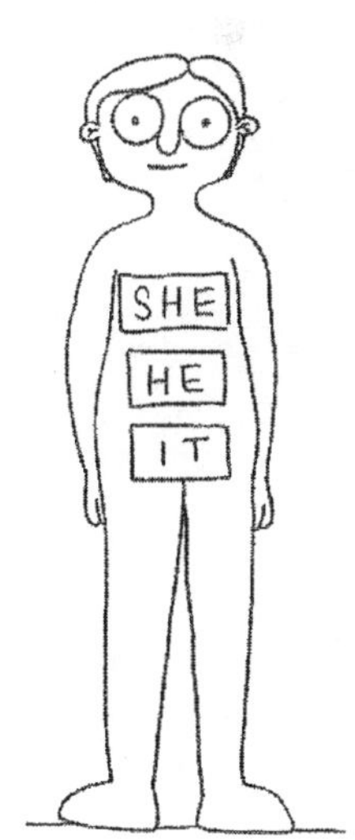

hoi polloi 1. I o' poo hill
2. I poll Ohio.
Ohio, an Akronism often confused with a poo hill, as stereotypic middle America represents the masses everywhere.

hors d'oeuvres Rush? Do serve o' "horse douvers".

haystack-fit needle finder: Heck, ya fire, let end, and sift.

Serendipity means searching for a needle in a haystack and instead finding a farmer's daughter. — *Anon.*

illiberally I really bill.

infuriated if "urinated!"

Infidelity, I? Tiny field!
Lechery, I? Cheerily!

intoxicated I tend a toxic ax-tied tonic adit-exit con.
I'm stealing this tongue-twister from the police who use it to test sobriety. Adit-exit is the doorway to oblivion, also known as

blottoed (bottle OD), or in a palindrome,
knur-drunk shit-faced, like a tree.

I surrender. *"Un derriers."*
Pardon my French. I believe this translates as "One kisses behind."

jubilation I, until a job!

Katrina anti-ark Where was Noah when we needed him?

King James Version (a slice ~~of~~ at history)
Jim ink-engraves, so joins meek ravings;
asks me, "No jive-grin mean virgins jokes!" Such as this one?:
immaculate conception: Ice it. No mate cum. No clap.

little toes "ole tittles"
Little toes are underachievers and should try harder! Or use Dr. Duck's™ **General Store** Toe Enlargers, his long-awaited nostrum for the digitally challenged. Painless, no pliers involved, no artificial sweeteners, 50% fat free.

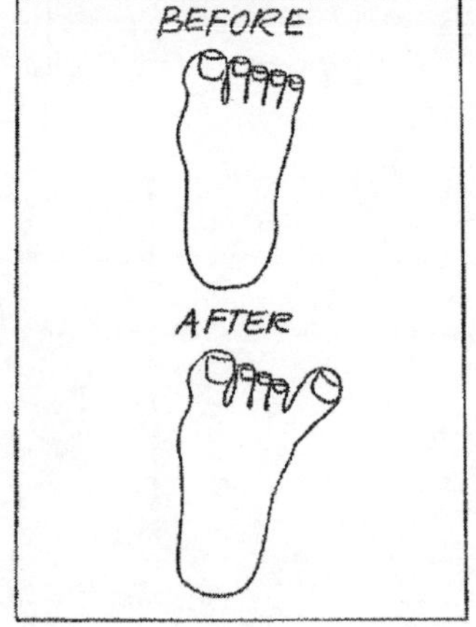

BE A FOOTY STAR!

"Leaved" (a myth)
Eve, Lad.
(Fig. it out for yourself.)
(Oh, okay, they "leaved" Eden.)

the lingam male "thing"
(Gin lameth the lingam.
"Ha, melting!")

loose end Needs loo. (Delhi belly?)

"Masturbates" (a taboo critter)
Bares at smut, a Mater's bust;
arm-beat tuss' at baser "must"† — † tussle; musth
rustles lusters' lustre's results rutless.
Wanked w/ naked ad, knew wad ken.
"Hand sex—near, fast and safer than sex!"

movie I move.
Ironically, this is an antonym: I don't move. I just sit there.
Not if it's a good movie! It moves you. (What, a bowel movie?)

New World Order WONDER^er WORLD
("Now" world erred. **Capitalism won,** now I'm a plastic.)

"Nous" or The Global Warning Debate
"O, *sun!*"
"No, *us!* So UN."
"Onus on US!"
"Un-so!"
(...un so on, us?) Goodbye, cool world.

nuclear physics unclear physics
Duly mispronounced "nuke-you-ler" by all Republicans since Eisenhower coined it.

"our son the dentist" The nitrous stoned?
Nitrous oxide, dental laughing gas and recreational drug.

oversexed eros vexed

Parlaiment (an unkind of essay)
Prat-ail men ram pat line (rampant lie), plant a mire: "I mar planet!" Politicians are a pain in my planet, my world and my butt.

politics "Pilot" (sic)
another sic joke

profit rip-oft

porcupine core pin-up ...for animal lovers
rhino horni ...for a different kind of animal lover

peter pan

pee'n trap

Solomon had 300 wives and 700 porcupines. — Dim Wit

"Quiet, Seas!" (a ~~short~~ wish-it-were-short story)
Queasiest sea quest I *quit* as see quiet sea's eases quit.

Republicans
Bun replicas snare public—**the masses**. ("Them asses?")

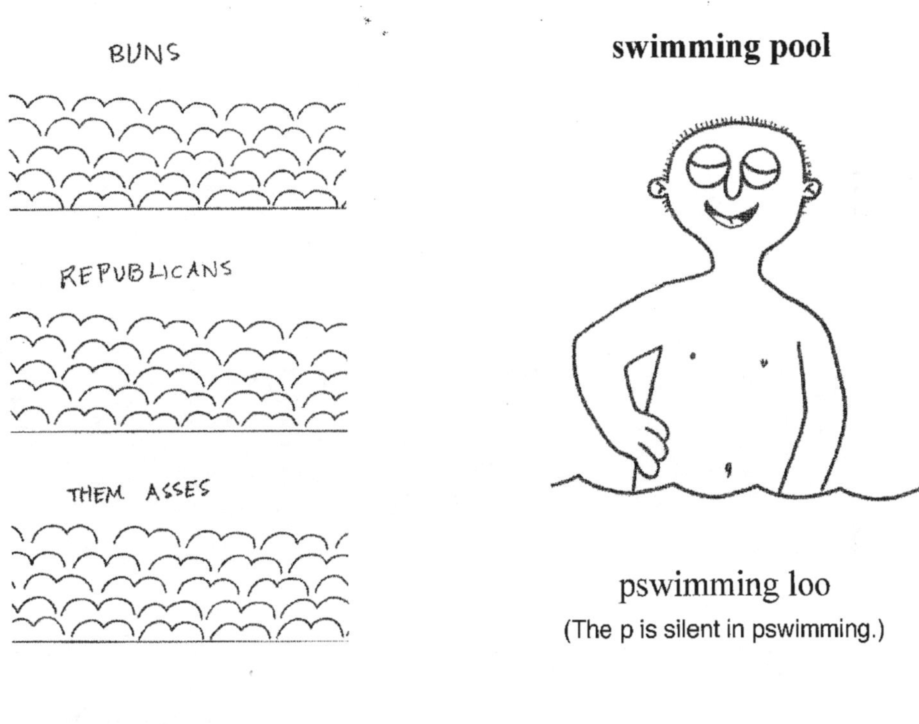

swimming pool

pswimming loo
(The p is silent in pswimming.)

sewer weers' "weres" and pooers "twoers" tours

slapstick sick splat Puns are so much more civil.

subservience bun-seer's vice
Skin colour DOES matter. The skin on your nose.

substitute use "butt-sit" the benchwarmer's moment of off-butt truth

Temperates...
1. temper eats,
2. eat tempers,
3. tame peters.

THE UPS AND DOWNS & INS AND OUTS OF LOVE

a long story—with mo' than one thrilling up-down, in-out episode

"Teen Sluts" (it begins)
Tense lust unsettles steel nuts, nettles us.

"Bothered" (it continues)
Hot breed be red hot to bed her bod there.

"Bedroom" (it climaxes)
Rode bomb*, roomed deb or mod boomer.
Reb-mood mod bore more bod, be m' door!
...Do mob 'er bod more, or mo' bed...

"Bedroom 2." (it anticlimaxes)
...Or mo'-bed-*bedroom!* (Bred mo' o' me brood.)*

"Bedroom 3." (it goes on, far too long after the anticlimax)
...Brood me brood, me reb mood doom: reb mode-rob broomed robedom, boredom-b'moored bedroom!

* Notes:

Bomb is a car, classic girl-getter. A mo'-bed bedroom is a self-reproducing entity, creating new bedrooms for a growing brood of kids. But in time this gets him down, causing him to brood over his uninspiring brood and his sterile stuck situation.

tadpoles leapdots ,‘ ’

tax loopholes plot o’ “ax-holes”

uniformity “You fit in, Mr.!”

villain ill ‘Ivan’ *(That’s terrible! — Ed.)*

whine “Win? *He?* When *I?*”

“You look great!” (You took LARGE.)
Being “great” ain’t so great, eh? Ask **the greatest human who ever lived**, as per the Guinness Book of Records, **J. B. Minnoch**, who topped out at 1400 lb or 635 kg!

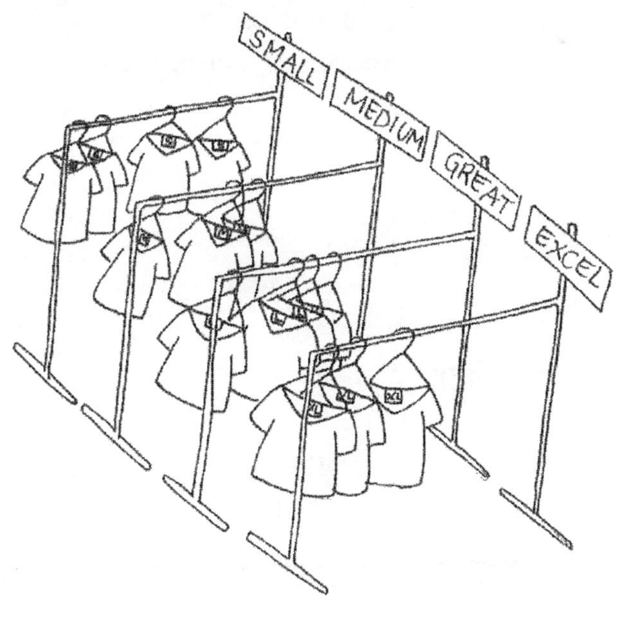

xenophile: "I help oxen;
"**xenophobe**, he bop oxen,
"**xenophobic** chop on ibex!"

HIRE EDUCATION

"Undergraduates"

(a long, sad story)

Undergraduates sat,
due "grandeur"
and "treasure",
dug drugs,
endure at a rust agenda,
ruder 'sugar etude'
and dude's argue rant.

"Postgraduate"

(it goes on, and on)

Postgraduate
pastured goat
adepts go a rut,
adapt,
get sour,
adopt true sag.

Chapter 2. **MAÑANAGRAMS**

These are anagrams to put (you) off till tomorrow. After a Word Ways article in Nov. 2004, it's an easy little quiz where one word of a sentence is replaced with an anagram of itself. Figure out which and restore the original sentence. Answers below. Piss poor parenthetical† comments are not hints but herrings.
† [$\text{PA}^{\text{REN}}{}_{\text{THETIC}}{}^{\text{AL}}$ = $^{\text{RENAL}}{}_{\text{PATHETIC}}$ = $^{\text{PISS}}{}_{\text{POOR}}$]

We're having martial problems, Doc. (Dubya, after Iraqshock?)

One good runt deserves another. (Little by Little)

God can't draw a straight Nile! (Think that's bad, look at the Yangtze.)

The snake filled her with adder. (Sounds kinky!)

Death awaits all abhorrent life. (Capital punishment?)

Terrorists, fanatics and other altruists should be ostracised. (OFF WITH THEIR HEADLINES!)

Watching TV airless suffocates me. (yet doesn't hold me breathless)

I'm nope-minded to new ideas. (Nope thanks, I thought at the office.)

He had a haggard, egad look about him. (From thinking too much?)

I was altered by the alarm clock. (an altered state of consciousness)

As the incestuous uncle said to his niece, "Come, sit on my pal."

There was a young lady from France
With a hole in the seat of her pants.
Not meant as a lure
But she had to be sure
To watch out for uncles and ants.

Answers: marital turn line dread earthborn ultraists serials open aged alerted lap.

Chapter 10. **PUN GENTLY**

("STATIC ANAGRAMS")

10A. **CHARADES**

I eat my peas with honey;
I've done it all my life.
It makes the peas taste funny,
But it keeps them on the knife. — *Anon.*

Most anagrams rearrange letters to create new words. **Charades** leave the letter order intact, like peas on honey, but create new phrases by changing the spacing or punctuation, etc. An example from 9A: **the masses** "Them asses?"

Here are three special types, all from *up/dn*:

Not here. No, there.

Synonyms. I present many such definitives—charades, anagrams, palindromes —in *up/dn* ('02) and in *Word Ways* (May'03 - Aug.'05, Nov.,'11).

A DOUBLE STANDARD IN NUMBERING

a standard 1, 2, 3 a 1st, a 2nd, a 3rd

A unique 'double charade' of interspersed letters and numerals.

Consumer goods cons 'um, ergo ODs.

This from chapter 5 runs them together into a sentence.

Dictionary definitions of anagrams would exclude charades, but they're so alike in spirit to anagrams, turning old letters into new words, that I see them as mere static anagrams. "Charades" is wordplay jargon not yet in dictionaries. Several of the following add regular anagrams to the charades to form polyanagrams.

bewitching Be w/ itching!

drug "Dr.—ug!!"

England En-gland! French opinion

frigid 1. f. rigid
frigid 2. (antonym) Frig ID: "Fig-rid, I'd frig."

gobbledegook Gob bled ego, OK?

innocents in no cents

hooker ho, “OKer”

malefactor male factor the Y chromosome

I'm pandering to feminists here. Hope I don't offend any male chauvinist pigs.

overmining ore O vermin in gore!

“Progress” PR ogress

Humanity... is like people packed in an automobile which is travelling downhill without lights at terrific speed and driven by a four-year-old child. The signposts along the way are all marked “Progress”. — Lord Dunsany

sea lords sod earls (anagram antonym)

Sea Lords sod Earls? Sod is Brit. slang for sodomise, a Lordly profession.

shackled shack-led severely domesticated

socialist So CIA list. What a charade! **A terror?** At error!

ugly *U*, G! L, Y? Say it aloud. What makes your big head so hard to look at?

"Women!"

Women	w/o men!!
w/ omen:	*Wo*, men!

This charade quartet (not necessarily related to the quartet pictured) is the manifesto of the feminist-terrorist organisation FEM—Forever Eliminate Men!—who seek a **Dam nation**.

If all the women left the country it would become a stagnation. — *Anon.*

But for an alternative view:

A woman's place is in the wrong. — *James Thurber*

Broadband Broad Band

Four half-pints make one quartet.

10B. **PUNC LIB CHARADES**

Mr. Oxley's been complaining about my punctuation, so I'm careful to get here before 9:00. — *Marilyn Monroe, Monkey Business*

I've breast-fed myself and it's not easy. — *Jane Garvey*

I woke up the other morning and found that everything in my room had been replaced by an exact replica. — *Steven Wright*

Most charades involve respacing the letters, creating new words. In contrast punc lib charades don't change the words *or* spacing, only the *punc*tuation (etc). Like punk kids in the old sense, liberated puncs break out of their cages and run freely among the words, wreaking havoc, totally changing if not reversing the meaning. The lowly comma wreaks the most havoc. An Australian oldie turns **Eats roots and leaves.** into **Eats, roots, and leaves.** ("Roots" means has sex in Australia.) (Or anywhere else for that matter if it's more convenient.)

You can easily infer what the original was in the one's where I give only the modified form. The first five below are other oldies to warm you to the idea. Many of the rest appeared earlier in *Word Ways* (Aug.,'09).

A Benny Hill classic:
Half the world doesn't know how; the other half lives.

Roger McGough puncs up a headline:
CONSERVATIVE GOVERNMENT. UNEMPLOYMENT. (FIGURES.)

From *Games* magazine: *Woman—without her, man is nothing.*

Anonymous, from my childhood:
Where do you think that'll get you, in the end? (ouch)

From a sportscast by Brian Johnston:
The bowler's Holding, the batsman's Willey.

It's not that simple mind, *you?*

I can't stand, being drunk.

It boggles, the mind

It staggers, the imagination.

You can lead a horse to water but you can't make it. Drink?
Lonely cowboy passes the bottle.

"I don't think. We're in *Kansas*, Toto!"
I shouldn't tease Kansas. They repealed that embarrassing Creationism rule.

He who can 'does' he who cannot. ("Teaches!")

Supports! **Supports?** [s^{UP}PORTS]

Would he cheat? He wouldn't know how, to be honest.
Would he cheat! He wouldn't know how to be honest.

I'll give you anything? You *wish!*

It's a sin to masturbate, boys.
Drop the comma and this call to boys becomes a call to girls. *(No hard feelings!)*

This one, for Rodney King, is a palindrome as well.

Espy LA, cop an apocalypse.
Espy LA cop—an apocalypse!

This one needs an anagram and a regular charade to set it up.

Hamburgers? "Ah, BM* urgers?" *Ha! MB urgers!*

---

* But BM doesn't mean Big Mac, means "shit".
(But "BM" doesn't mean Big Mac means shit!)
God forbid. So, does a BM a day keep the MB away? Not if BM means Big Mac. (Interestingly, "means shit" means "doesn't mean shit".)

Here's a pithy double-take on this book's title:

How to Double: the Meaning of Life.

Compare the classic anagram by Enavlicm (*Enigma,* 1917): **families:** life's aim. But the punc lib could equally refer to personal growth, or to aggrandisement.

Earth life was up and running, well before we arrived on the scene.
Earth life was up and running well, before we arrived on the scene!
Goodbye, cool world.

What? Is this world coming to? I dearly hope so!

Chapter 11. Palindromes

IS A PUN EVIL? LIVEN UP, AS I!

Alas, poor Yorlik, I knew him backwards. — *Anon.*

It's 1-1, an exact reversal of the score on Saturday. — *DimWit*

What do you get when you play New Age music backwards?
New Age music. — *Anon.*

Come early if you want a seat at the back. — *on synagogue door*

Extremes meet, as the whiting said with its tail in its mouth.
— *Thomas Hood*

a swallowtail struggling to make ends meet

11A. **PALINDROME PUNUP**

Palindromes (pals) are the brainchildren of palindromists, a retrograde species. We're of two opposing types, **firm** and **"Mr. If "**. I'm a shameless wannabe of both, looking for some **hah-hah** or **heeheeh** from backward thinking either way it comes. Two digs at us compulsive palindromists from chapter 3:

Ginterpretnig is our effort to explain something while under the ginfluence.
Spontanenatnops is the involuted result when we try to be spontaneous.

We're the kind of people who name our children **Anna, Bob, Dud, Eve, Gig, Idi** *(surely not!)*, **Judge Gduj, Llewell, Nan, Otto, Tulsa Slut, Tut, Viv** or **Wow.** That last one is for those who have already used up all the other names.

A friend of mine confused her Valium with her birth control pills.
She had fourteen children but didn't give a shit. — *Joan Rivers*

Unbold titles and notes (in a different typeface) are not part of the **palindromes,** which are **all bold**. Some more than others. Palindromes can also be reversals of words or syllables rather than of letters. A few are satirical GNOMES IN DROMES you may not find at all funny. Or you might find them **laff-off offal,** which I'd accept as a compliment, being hard up.

I can live for two months on a good compliment. — *Mark Twain*

palindrome I'm polar end-on-mid relap, an "imploder".

Neat definition of a palindrome, not by a palindrome but by its cousin a polyanagram.

palindrome: Pun-up 'em? Or dn I lap?

Introspective palindromes like this can have a positive or a negative effect, *up* or *dn.*

<u>THE DESERTER</u>

Made NOT! sign. 'I'm mellow AWOL lemming. I stoned am,'

<u>THE STUDENT'S DILEMMA</u>

books v. skoob

"Scoob" is slang for a marijuana joint, a drug capable of changing its own spelling.

<u>GETTING AHEAD BY GETTING BEHIND</u>

butter up: up 'er butt (butt = a fat tub)

<u>CYANICAL DEFINITION OF MARRIAGE</u>

sex-insane vow woven as nixes

Do you swear you'll never look at another again? "Not ever!" Never? "Well, hardly ever." Hardly? "Well, not *ALWAYS*. Not *EVER!* Like I said."

<u>GETTING PREGNANT FOR KICKS</u>

gamomania: A mom again!

The kicks are from the womb. Gamomania = gamete-obsessed (a coinage). Not a true palindrome; "a mom aGain" is a circular or out-of phase reversal of Gamomania.

SAVE THE DOUGH, DOE!

doe: deer's dear

—or dear deer's dough?

November/June romance and caution,
"Is he only after your money, dear deer doe?"

DOE-DOE

Two does recreate the dodo in an early go at bioengineering.

AFFLUENT EFFLUENT

Go bare West sewer—a bog!
Beware Era web.

A LEAKED STORY (Dutch Headline)

DIKE—VAST SAVE, KID!

DRY HUMOUR

"Gorgon!" (no grog)

Pal version of the incorrect joke, *"What's the difference between a dog and a fox?" "About six drinks."* And six Gorgon's Dry Gins™ can turn gorgons **"Gorgeoush!"**

'NO MISTEAK ABOUT IT!'

'Detail *at-error* retaliation?' 'No, I tail *a terror*, retaliated!'

This was composed while I was Dubya's speechwriter. (haha) Funny how it comes back on itself like a palindrome should.

Mind never *knows* it, what it "knows". Never mind.

POST OFFICE ENIGMA

parcel, bad: "AER NUGRAM O VRIL GYKKY GLIR VOMARG..." (unreadable crap)

The sender carelessly forgot to mention which planet it was addressed to.

HOLLYWOOD SCOOP!

Oogamy Magoo

The full name of this famous personage is now revealed. He prefers to be called "Mister" because Oogamy (reproduction by egg and sperm of very different size) stresses his smallness. "Such a tiny and wiggly baby," his parents must've thought.

Football is a fertility festival. Eleven sperm trying to get into the egg. I feel sorry for the goalkeeper. — *Björk*

"IT'S A SILLY GENTILE THING"

Yoyo yoga for/of a goy, oy-oy!

TM™

Apparently, if you play country and western music backwards, your lover returns, your dog comes back and you cease to be an alcoholic. — *Linda Smith*

11B. PAIRINDROMES

This special type of palindrome, introduced in the Feb.'08 *Word Ways*, gives a combined meaning to unrelated word pairs that happen to be spelling reversals.

desserts-stressed

Overweight, diabetic, hypertense–*and yet*
stressed desserts!

Snub buns.

Celibacy? Or just an Atkins diet?

lap pal

A child, a toy dog, a cat, a shotgun, a pet cobra, a doll, or (oh oh) a
bonk knob (!)
If the latter, the doll might be a lap dancer—or a French niece.

nuts stun the unkindest blow of all

"Ow!" wo response to nuts stun – and **"woow"** for a time thereafter

Chapter 12.

A SORDID LETTER PLAY

A ninny is someone willing to look after children. — *Anon.*

It is bad form to sit with your legs over the arm of your char. — *Anon.*

The train now arriving on Platforms 6, 7, 8 and 9 is coming in sideways. — *Anon.*

Big Fleas Have Little Fleas
That Sit Upon And Bite 'Em,
And Little Fleas Have Lesser Fleas,
And So Ad Infinitum. — *Jonathan Swift*

There are perhaps as many ways to fuck around with letters and meanings as there are ways to dissect a flea, *ad infinitum*. The many varieties of abuse in the rest of this book are even uglier and often more violent than mere anagrams, charades and palindromes. For instance one can *behead* a **Pirate** just to make him **irate**. **Terrorists** are people who lose their heads and become **errorists.**

Or take the first letters of the 21 words in the Swift quotation and rearrange them into the anacrogram **"Ah, subhabits! flea, fla, fl, f, ...** "

Another acrostic:

arsehole: a really **s**tupid **e**arfucker **h**azarding **o**ur **l**evel **e**motions

Crimes in the following chapters include single letter alterations, pig latin, space and shape and numeral manipulation, turning keyboard characters into pictures (something everyone loves to play at) and into enigmatic codes or rebuses. If you find these categories unintelligible, just *unread* this paragraph down to here. Done? Now read on blindly. Trust me. I personally guarantee that this whole book is absolutely error free, except for this sentence.

12A. **ODDS AND ENDS**

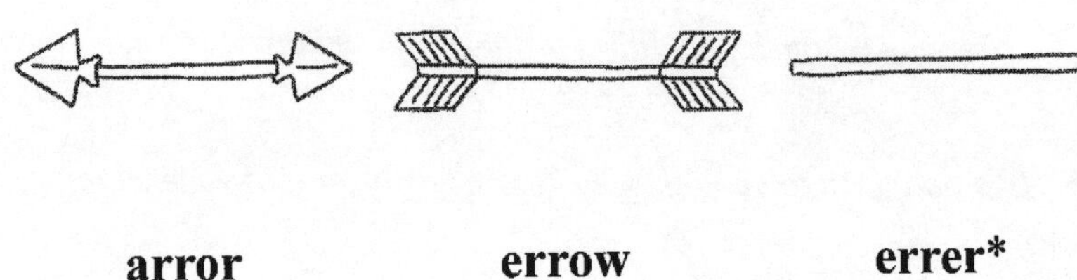

arror **errow** **errer***

* ERRER is a word that describes *you* if you thought it was an ERROR.

Peer Peer peer.

HOUSE OF LORDS LATRINE DUTY

LITERARY NARCISSISM

This sentence is concerned solely with its own ~~end ends ending close closing closure termination finish conclusion denoument eventuation discontinuance quit finalisation resolution culmination consummation winding-up demise passing expiration expiry quietus Waterloo curtains death obliteration finalisation period full-stop~~ end.

LITERARY PRAGMATISM

~~this sentence would make good barbwire~~

LETTERARY WISDOM (with ewer indulgence)

The plural of **U** is **Us**,
for what I call **ME** is a reflection of '**EM**
and the flip side of **WE** — and all reflect **EW!**

EGO TRIPPING

Taxi Driver: *"Where to, bud?"*
Jilted Lover: *"Drive off a cliff. I'm committing suicide."* — *Anon.*

12B. **WORD LADDERS**
WORILADDERS
WORIDADDERS
WORLD ADDERS

In a word ladder each step differs from the next by one letter. (Thus the above title sequence *isn't* a word ladder except in name and appearance.) Ladders were invented by Lewis Carroll in a type he called "doublets" that connect opposites at the two extremes. Some of those here are doublets. I mostly follow Carroll's formula of leaving letter order intact, but a few rearrange the letters at one or more steps. Fanciful TITLES and comments are not part of the letter play but may help in interpreting it. Most of these, minus titles, are from the 2002 *Word Ways*. They are primarily little stories or essays rather than gags but you may find them amusing. The first example is quasi-historical.

WAS CAESAR A LATIN LOVER?

Veni,
vini,
vidi,
vici.

Latin for "*I came, I wined, I saw* (her), *I conquered.*"
(Almost. Actually he conqued out from all the wine.)

ARE ADS LETHAL? **Ay, at an ad am as at an ax!**

THE TRUTH ABOUT HEROICS **I rave "brave"? Crave grave!**

DEFINITIVE INCEST

kin sin: "Sib lib" lit, hit hot cot.

GONORRHEA (a doublet)

Fun fan fad fed bed, bid bod bud bad:
Sad lad had mad wad, wed wee **woe**.

THE OLD T&A

"Lust bust, butt."

Or as Punc Lib would say, **Lust, bust butt** for it.

T & A

THE TURN OF THE SCREW

Screwed,
Shrewed,
Screwed!
(*Not* shrewd.)

shuffle scuffle souffle the art of baking anagrams

12B2. **VOWEL CASCADES**

These are five-word ladders which run through the vowels in one slot, forward or backward. The first and third (pairs) are spelling or letteral cascades: a e i o u. The other two are phonic cascades: eh ee eye oh ewe.

Bad BED bid bod bud. — *Bag*, beg, big bog BUG!

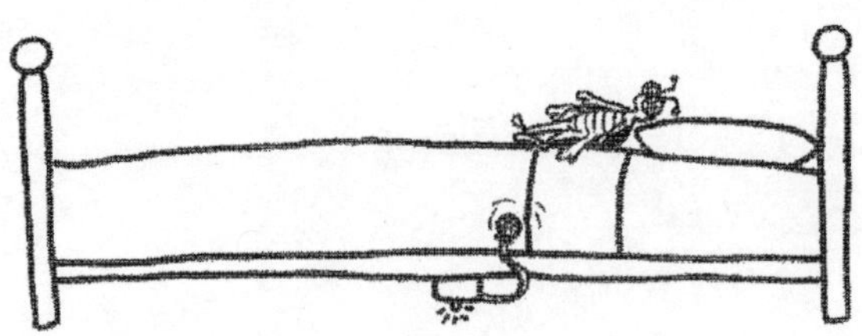

BED BUGS

Everyone in the Swiss army owns a Swiss army knife.
That's why no one messes with Switzerland. — *Cheers*

PICNIC IN A PAY TOILET

Paid,
Peed,
Pied,
Poe'd,
Poo'd / "pew!"ed.

Wasn't there a fad once to see how many people could squeeze into a pay toilet, eat pies and read **POE**try together? I believe peeing, pooing and pewing were optional.

THE DOCTOR'S OWN MEDICINE (a palindrome)

Dum Dom dim dem dam mad med mid mod mud.

The doctors are stupefied by both the champagne and the times.

God's plan made a hopeful beginning,
But man spoiled his chances by sinning.
We trust that the story
Will end in God's glory,
But, at present, the other side's winning. — *NYTimes Mag., 1946*

WHAT, IS THIS WORLD COMING TO?

Sane scene sign sown soon.

"This insane world," we keep hearing, "is about to wake up."

Our problem is not insanity so much as feeble-minddness,
a refusal to think things out at all. We watch [TV] instead.
— *Auberon Waugh*

12B3. **WORD STOOLS**

Word stools are not excrement (I argue) but mere <u>one-step ladders</u>, two words or coinages that differ by one letter but are otherwise unrelated. Until now.

Ducking for apples—change one letter and it's the story of my life.
— Dorothy Parker

Sex is just one damp thing after another. *— Anon.*

I have learned the difference between a cactus and a caucus.
On a cactus the pricks are on the outside. *— Morris K. Udall*

Jean Harlow: How do you do, Mar-got?
Margot Asquith: The "t" is silent, as in Harlow.

Business Dusiness

Dusiness is motion sickness from job stress, head spinning from spin spinning—or the inevitable result when a business's B head is replaced by a D-head? Saying the words two ways gives this executive slogan:

"When BUSYNESS = DIZZYNESS... BOOZINESS = DOOZINESS!"

gung-ho DAVY DUNGBEETLE

LEAPING **LEOPARDS**
LEOTARDS

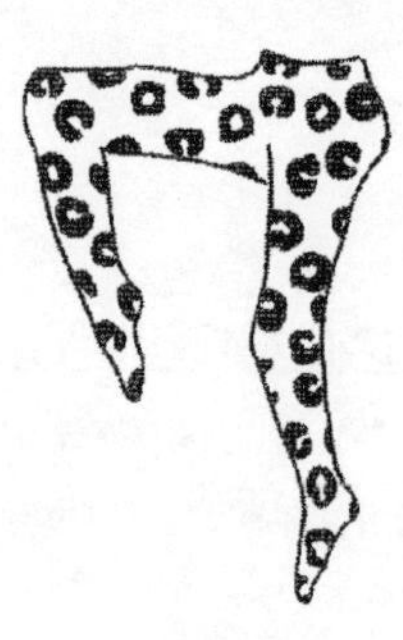

(a topless dancer)

A MINOR REVISION TO THE MODERN WEDDING VOWS

live → like

"...so long as you both shall ~~live~~ like." Or, "s.l.a.y.b.s. ~~live~~ **love**."

more stocking, more shocking

I've often wondered, when shorts were shocking, were short shorts less shocking? A less material affront, like the bikini?

Pates? Nates? Heads or tails?

> *"If you're torn between our date and your phrenology meeting tonight," she said, "flip a coin."* — *Anon.*

TWO EXTREME VIEWS, or YOU CAN'T HIDE FROM BIG BRO

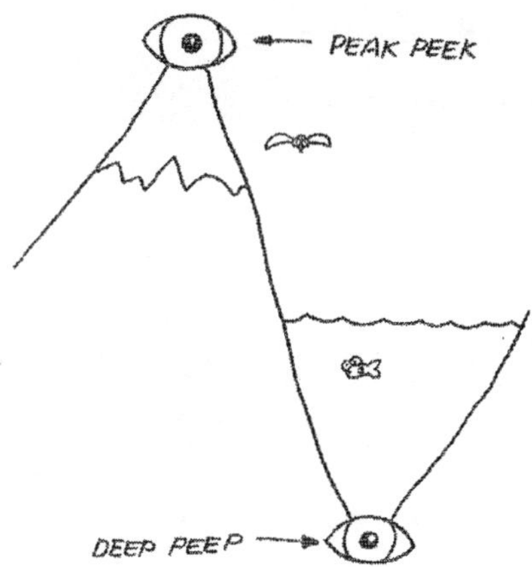

prat's prate Talking thru the terminal orifice; aka farting around.

taste of heaven taste of heavin' Opposites unless you overindulge.

12C. **IGPAY @ INLAY**

The title is pig latin for Pig Latin sake. Compulsively I turn it into yet another way to tease puns or funs out of word abuse. (Pig Latin should not be confused with Pigletin, the language spoken by Igletpay in *Anyway, the Ooo Pay!*) Most of these are from the May 2006 *Word Ways*.

Coke, OK!
You owe me big time for this one, Coca-Cola! And Colombia!

fart: Art fey **waft**, aft-way.

lass "Ass—lay!" says the male **chauvinist** ova-nest-shy igpay.

pew You pay. coin-op religion (or a recently used pay toilet)

pill Ill? Pay!
"Free market" medicine is a hard pill to swallow.

puppet "up it" pay

As you know, all a dummy gets paid is a fist up its behind. Some gays would say he's no dummy.

silly Illy say. Sick humour? Mental illness? Moi?

LIFE WITHOUT RUTH
"**Win!** 'In' way. **Winny** *any* way*!*"

12D. **HIGHER MATHS**

TOWARDS AN ALTERNATIVE NUMBER SYSTEM

Before unloading some number puns on you, I present two pages of selections from the multi-author *Essentials of Pneumath* for your intellectual inflation.

"If you had five pounds," said the teacher, "and I asked you for three, how many would you have then?"
"Five," said young McTavish. — *Anon.*

...eleven goals, exactly double the number he scored last season.
— *Alan Perry*

A man has five children. Half of them are boys. Is that possible?
No. *Yes, it is. The other half are also boys.* — *Benny Hill*

Two out of every one people in Ireland are schizophrenic. — *Jimeoin*

Whatever women do they must do twice as well as men to be thought half as good. Luckily, this is not difficult. — *Charlotte Whitton*

A man does not have to be a bigamist to have one wife too many.
— *The Farmer's Almanac*

I once dated a guy so dumb he couldn't count to 21 unless he was naked. — *Joan Rivers*

An old lady was overheard saying, on the introduction of decimalisation: "I think they should have waited until all the old people were dead." — *Anon.*

I started out with nothing and I've still got most of it left. — *Anon.*

It's clearly a budget. It's got a lot of numbers in it. — *Dubya*

We divided the house equally. She got the inside, I got the outside.
— *Anon.*

"Her legs are without equal." "You mean they know no parallel?"
— *Anon.*

There are three kinds of people: those who can count and those who can't. — *Anon.*

Gross ignorance is 144 times worse than ordinary ignorance. — *Anon.*

He who slings mud usually loses ground. — *Adlai Stevenson*

When it comes to giving, some people stop at nothing. — *Yiddish proverb*

He's deadly 10 times out of 10, but this wasn't one of them. — *Peter Jones*

So that's 57 runs needed... in 11 overs—and it doesn't need a calculator to tell you that the run rate required is 5.1818...
— *Norman De Mesquita*

I am on two diets at the moment because you don't get enough to eat on one. — *Peter Sissons*

I know that two and two make four—though I must say if by any sort of process I could convert two and two into five it would give me much greater pleasure. — *Lord Byron*

Dear Lord (if I may call you by your first name): || + || = \V/ (Roman) or 5 (Arabic). You're welcome. My honour. Now you can quit turning over numbers in your grave and get on with decomposing peacefully.

69 Latin* *sex* figures at odds and ends

"The square root of 69 is 8 something." — Anon. But a 69 'root' isn't square!

96 69 'over', sleeping, smoking or puking.

* Latin lovers think ***sex*** means **six**. Kinky.

prisom where naughty photons are incarcerated

Inprisomable offences include participation in porn, forgery, plagiarism, libel, fraud and optical illusions. "Optical illusions may be predominantly harmless, but if they were legalised it would send the wrong message."

PRISOM

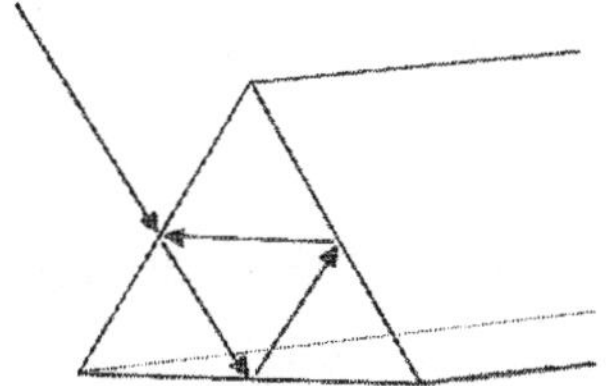

RECTANGLE

2 HALF-TRUTHS = 1 TRUTH?

Yes, this is how politicians achieve credibility.

A CUTE ANGEL

When I eventually met Mr. Right, I had no idea that his first name was "Always." — *Rita Rudner*

If a man speaks in the forest and there is no woman around to hear him, is he still wrong? — *Jerry Dennis*

Double negatives are a complete no-no. — *Anon.*

0 + 0 = 00

Infinity arises out of the collision of two voids. A double negative is a positive. Chaos theory sees it in reverse, "For infinity nothing happens twice!"

SELF-DEFINING DIGITS

zer0	**one**	**tv vo**	**threee!**	**f o u r**
fiVe	**sIIIIX**	**7even**	**ei8ht**	***n*IX** (nein)

nothing *n*=0 thing (charade)

"I'm number one!" *You're next to* ***zero!***

TWO ANAGRAMS

two to "w" Say it out loud. *Twice.*

Illuminate "two-faced." A 'low' in multifaceted.

CORRECTION: ***Two and two equal two!*** Two = two = TWO = II = 2

A Fourgone Conclusion:
012356789.

FOURCLOSURE

4 ⇨ 4

12E. **PUNCS**

Puncs, aka emoticons, are smart-alecky drawings made with keyboard characters, especially **punc**tuation marks. I've used a few in earlier acts. Viewed sideways they are common playthings. I prefer them upright as in text, so that a smiling face (-: becomes a recumbent idiot or a blissfully retired President.

coy beauty ~~~
{'''^'''}~

junior beauty ”-”

snowman with sword (..)
(by Calvin & Hobbes?) (_†>

surprised lady { ! ! }
(I'd be too. A sword??) \ 0 /

surprised dog ! !
or horse ^

dog in goggles @—@
(Surprised?) P

"Meet you at the Y," .(Y).
said the cootie to the fly.

Hallowe'en /o o\
or KKK attire

primate (O ∞ O)
(and my girlfriend) (—)

walrus (¡ ¡)

Tweetie (0◇0)

Ganesh (o j o)

bat, mosquito, or a nosey Hindu ^¡^

weeper, or staring daggers, or cross-eyed {†..†}

1. two shrews or birds quarrelling ·><·
   (Lighten up, Anil, maybe they're kissing. Ed.)
2. or one hungry reptile eyeing them
   (Lighten up again, maybe it's just curious, or wary.)

cockeyed frog, or monkey holding a baby ≤%≥

self-fellatio, or fell asleep meditating ≤∂≥

borer and boree {°< ....):

The boree (right) has fallen over in agony.

man in balcony at a striptease “

what he's staring at “

orchestra pit member ”

This scenario also works with the numbers 66 and 99. 666 is a she-devil. "The number of the beast" is a typo meant to be "the number of the breast".

hook among the fishies <· ¿ <· <·

as in "cat among the pigeons"

Zen painting: ( ) ∧

"Rising Sun over Mt. Fuji"

12E2. **SOME REAL ALPHABETICAL CHARACTERS**

These pseudo-etymologies turn typescript into pictures, as in chapter 12, but not by arranging them. They rearrange the mind of the beholder instead. The complete alphabet is in *Word Ways*, Feb.,'09.

letter	what it originally depicted
A	Venus Williams awaiting a serve, rear view, arse-up
B†	Dolly Parton, top view *(Is that † a dagger in her hand?)*
D	half an empty capsule
H	coitus erectus, *highly* diagrammatic
I	naughty photo of same, side view (after Roger Price)
J	umbrella in extreme wind
M	anorexic at an ob-gyn exam
U	*Here's* where the other half of that capsule went!
W	A giant Wabbit is about to gwab you from above.
X	ménage à quatre

† Too many boob jokes finally got to her? Help! I'll be next! Or is the daggar just a footnoting that the letter **B** was created in **D**olly **P**arton's honour by fusing **D** and **P**. It also stands for BOOB, a self-depicting word, a frontal view flanked by two top views.

I was the first woman to burn my bra—it took the fire department four days to put it out. — *Dolly Parton*

12F. **BBs** (rebuses)

A BB is a rebus—of **rebus** (Re-B us). Rebuses are pictograms and other visual enigmas. They are usually given as teasers but I'll explain them on the spot to spare you the brain drain pain. If you prefer to make a puzzle of it, simply cover up the right hand column of answers with a heavy weight. Many of these are homophonic puns as in volume III. Mostly from the Feb.'03 *Word Ways*.

$ giant Serpent on a ra||road track saying "Don't tread on me."

This monetary theory doesn't work on the common single-bar dollar sign. A snake on only one track is not big enuf to make the slogan credible. Where did that other bar go in the common fonts anyhow? Removing it is like taking a star away from the flag! Those font people should give back all those bars. What'd they have in mind, trying to pass them off as half-dollars?

(I searched my computer's many offerings and found only two honest fonts that don't steal one of the bars. As you're dying to know, the one here is STKaiti.)

Apo**11**o	man-in-the-moon logo
CNN	seein' double A regular practice?
f	little left to see
EEfEuEEnEgEEuDZsDZ	penicillin attack: "At ease disease, [8 Es, DZs] there's a fungus among us."
.** **G** . * .	gastronomical

Behind every successful man stands a surprised mother-in-law. — *HHH*

HHH the dark H's

The lit 60s actually—'lit' in several senses. **H**ubert **H**oratio **H**umphrey in 1968 ran for President against Nixon. It was two Vices trying to make a Virtue of themselves.

LF HA! a semi joke—LF your HA off! (Hope you're not antisemi?)

((m)) immodest

MCE MCE MCE three blind mice

MUSA emanation

A banana (*Musa*) republic?

nnnnnnnnnnnnnnnnnnn noodles

See the resemblance? Think Noodle Falls.

ON ⇆ NO a self-defeating preposition

another victim of palindromania

O **O** o O ◻ Ȯ o 0 o Ô **0**

◑ **0** O O ○ ◙ *O O* ◻ *0* ovaries

It takes all types to run a species.

RPRAIRNR pain in the Rs

SQ	"Askew?" ask you.
T H E	Everything! *The* beginning, *the* middle and *the* end.
Tl	thallic symbol *(Doesn't look like a thallus to me. Ed.)*
world	It's a small world, isn't it?
X	exemplified
ZZZZZZZZZZZZ	1. a long nap 2. zero (zee row) 3. zealot (zee a lot)
~~**333**~~	not half bad
0123 56789	Wherefour art thou? Thou art been fourgone since chapter 12D.

12F2. **LETTERAL WORDS**

Letteral words, aka gramograms, are also rebuses, words spelt phonetically by letters. Here are four dozen. The answers are alphabetical across. Read each character separately (except the 10s), perhaps out loud or varying the emphasis. Translations are given below if required. Or not.

HU!	AGNC	HNC	NLG6
NIL8	NE1	SN9	SSS
AV8R	O8	OA	BD
B10	B4	B9	DK
DV8	LMN8	MN8	NV
SKP	Sπ	XL	XXX
4A	4C	GOD6	EBGB^2
LO	(LO2U2!)	IC	MNCT
NDN	N8	N10CT	IV
JL	OBDNC	PNO	CD
6S	10US	YL	Y10
ELO	EN?	ES!	UBUT!

TRANSLATIONS (Ignore these if you're a happy person.)
achoo! (sneeze) Aegean Sea agency analgesics
annihilate anyone asinine assesses
aviator await away beady or bidi
beaten before benign decay
deviate eliminate emanate envy
escapee espy excel exec's sex
foray foresee geodesics heebie-jeebies
hello (hello to you too!) icy, I see immensity
Indian innate intensity ivy
jail obediency piano seedy (music?)
success tenuous while or wile whiten
yellow Yen, Ian? Yes. You bea-u-ty!

12F3. TYPES CRYPT

ABCDTV.

GZ*B*DTV!

These are adult letterals. Not naughty, just grown up, not words but complete sentences or phrases. The one at right reads

> Abie see the TV.
> ...Jeez, he *be* the TV.

Z may be said zee (as here) or zed. Punctuation is just an aid, usually not pronounced.
Exceptions: * = asterisk; # = number
/ = bar; [= bracket; ^ = caret; ; = semicolon
II = i's, eyes (otherwise read each letter)

"CDII? CMNDX?"

"See the eyes? See 'em in the eggs?"

"L,ICMNOX."
"OSARNDX!
FNUNE¢?
2IF2/O1N[4U?"

"Hell, I see them in no eggs."
"Oh yes they are in the eggs!
Haven't you any sense?
Do I have to borrow one and break it for you?"

FNE1SQI810Q.
I8NN*N*RX.
NI8A^ND^;
12NE1^?

If anyone asks you, I ate, thank you. I ate an hen *and* her eggs. And I ate a carrot, and the carrot's in me colon. Doesn't anyone care at all? [caret tall]

IFA#LO.U2?

I have an umbrella. You too?

CZA? 4Q,USO!	Seize the day? Fork you, you asshole!
IM*∞?	I am asked to risk everything?
OK,UN,QTπ. ZZ!	Okay, you win, cutie pie. It's easy!
"P(7)O8,7," ZI.	"Peace (Heaven) awaits, Evan," said I.
"4728!" ZR7.	"Force Heaven to wait!" said arse Evan.
"U1284FRNFR!" ZI.	"You want to wait for ever and ever!" said I.

BIBLIOFILE IV. **Future Tittles 4**

The Fantastic Four vs. The Terrible Twos
The world is overrun with 2-year old terrorists. Can our superhero quartet cope?

How to Solve Marital Problems with Logarithms
Thickly applied mathematics. Preface by the Chair of the Log Table Factory.

The Picasso Code
At last! Make sense of those enigmatic pictures.

The Genetics Lecturers Who Described a Double Helix While Diving into the Grand Canyon
Spiralling revelations about the chain of life. Greater love hath no geneticist than this, a 'suicide dive bombers' pact between two DNA-lover lovers as a publicity stunt to promote helical awareness. Pix & transcripts of the dive lectures.

Fatland, by a Round
The story of how a robust diet expanded a 1D mind into a 3D spheroid. It's an expanded sequel to Edwin Abbott's 1884 2D adventure, *Flatland, by a Square.*

Tips on Deciding How Long to Wait Between Breaths

Constipation in the Lower Semicolon, or Don't Forget to Dot Your Commas Improve your wellbeing with freely flowing grammar.

The Tenuous Relationship Between Bureaucratic Red Tape and the Speed of Light A statistical investigation that will help you pass the time while waiting for light to reach the bureaucrat.

HOW TO DOUBLE THE MEANING OF LIFE

Act V

PROSE AND CONS

> *Mums — after your kids have mastered spelling with Alphabetti Spaghetti, buy a tin of the normal stuff so they can practice joined-up writing.* — *Viz*

The previous four Acts consisted mostly of dictionary style lists of critters. I've since learned joined-up writing, so this final act can stick to whole sentences and paragraphs. But my devious purposes remain the same, pun fun peppered with satire. It's divided into genres, as seen (if you're lucky) in the table of contents.

THE THREE WISE GUYS DISCOVER TIME TRAVEL

Don't let the masks fool you. They're really fun guys.

Act V CONTENTS

Chapter 13. **NEO-TRUISMS**

It's a strange world of language in which skating on thin ice can get you into hot water. — *Franklin P. Jones*

I like its independent attitude.
Let no one call it a ***duck-billed platitude.*** — *Ogden Nash*

Dear Ogs, I *was* calling my Neo-truisms "duckbill platitudes" until I came across your edict. Sorry. And damn your eyes for stealing my pun—even before I was born! *(Apologies again. I've just hacked into the government's hush-hush Minds database and discovered that in fact I'm the 3918th person to think of that pun. You were 3rd.)*

He who laughs lasts. —*Anon.*

Time wounds all heels. — *Groucho Marx (attrib.)*

Neo-truisms are new "old saws", revisionism perpetrated on common sayings and idioms by various hilarious nefarious devices. The above two classics of the form use foreshortening and word swap plus homophone. Other devices used include hybridisations and mixed proverbs, substitutions, mutations and sillifications. More old examples follow. And still more in *Word Ways*, Aug.'04.

People who live in glass houses shouldn't. — *Philip Cohen*

Familiarity breeds. — *Laugh-In*

Folks, just keep those cards and letters. — *Laugh-In*

Virtue is its own punishment. — *Aneurin Bevan*

Vice is its own reward. — *Quentin Crisp*

Some things have got to be believed to be seen. — *Ralph Hodgson*

Freeze, motherstickers, this is a fuck up! — *Florida bank robber*
[what irony as he fled, embarrassed and empty-handed]

Misery begins at home. — *Jan Ackerson*

Time is but skin deep. [an anti-aging creme ad?] — *J. A.*

Outside every thin girl is a fat man trying to get in.
— *Katharine Whitehorn*

A fool and his words are soon parted. — *William Shenstone*
(Okay, I confess. On and on.)

Cleanliness is next to impossible. — *Mary Youngquist/Harry Hazard*

You can't teach an old dog card tricks. — *M. Y./ H. H.*

Never judge a book by its movie. — *J. W. Egan*

Avoid cliches like the plague. — *Lawrence Dorfman*

In these examples, as in my own critters to follow, the twists usually result in real ideas if not "new truisms". But the gnomes are infiltrated by frivolous goblins, naughty trolls and impish imps. The few that combine insight and humour I dub **wisdom cracks.** They are simultaneously wisecracks *and* remarks that might open a crack in one's skull. (Ouch.) On the other hand, if you find my wisdom laughable, the laugh is on me. Gratis.

Anagrams, normally my friends, also turn on me here and say of my posturings:
Neotruisms? ie, Nostrums! **Wisdom cracks?** Sick word scam!

Ever since Newton things
have been going downhill.

Many hands take a light load.

Honesty is the beset policy.

Miser loves Company. ♥

Love is a blind.

Man cannot be bred alone.

Love thy neighbour as thy wife.

One man's meat makes Jack a doll boy.

The price of liberty is eternal virginity.

Actors speak louder than nerds.

Books are deceiving.

What's dumb cannot be undumb.

You shall know the truth and the truth shall make you sick.

"Sufficient unto the day" begins at forty.

Boogers can't be chewers. (After a certain age.)

If it looks like a duck, walks like a duck and talks like a duck, *duck!* It might be that infamous quack, *Dr. Duck!*
Read of his exploitations at the Dealy Deli in the Feb.'05 *Word Ways*.

DR. DUCK and his bodyguard, BETTER DUCK

Sticks and stones may break my bones but words will never fail me.

Nothing succeeds like succession.

Opportunity runs in families.

There is honour among well-placed thieves.

Get it down in blank and white.
This is how governments deal with unfavourable reports.

US Government is based on a system of checks and bounces.

If at first you don't succeed, try, try a gin!

"Quit while you're a head." hippee drop-out slogan

Don't hide your light under a bustle.
Casanova's advice to eighteenth century ladies

l'Oeuf makes the world go round. Egg reproduction is the spin.

A man without Religion is like a slave without a master.

Longevity is the best medicine.

All things come to those who live forever.

As you make your story so must you lie in it.
I don't lie much anymore. It requires too good a memory.

See no evil, hear today, gone tomorrow, all's right with the world.

What you don't know can't help you.

Nothing is certain but death in Texas.
Particularly for convicted criminals.

It is never too late to forget the Alamo.

Cogito ergo cogito.
I think therefore I think.
Another meaning for **chasing tail**,
chasing thoughts around in my head.

Good clothes open all doors.
—Anon.

Circular reasoning
is its own reward.

The pot thickens.
Stewed again? Or waisted?

Taste makes waist.
Whatsoever a man rippeth
that shall he also sew.
A stitch in time saves embarrassment.

Some things are easier said than antidisestablishmentarianism.

"One rotten apple spoils the Garden!" expels Adam.

Every mirror has a silver lining.

A stitch in time goes away.

A rose by another name would no longer be a rose. It'd be that other thing.

Worchester, like most colleges, does not admit dogs. The Dean's dog, Flint, has thus been officially declared a cat by the governing body. — Anon.(Oxon)

When the tough get going, the going gets tough.

Rats deserve a sinking ship. (Eco rats., that is.)

Man is the messer of all things.

If you play with fire you get greenhouse gases.

"Lord what fuels these mortals be." — Shakespire

" The sky is fouling! The sky is fouling!"
The sky is fowling?

Assassination is the sincerest form of flattery.

Whoso profits from war is worth a pound of curare.

A penny saved is a penny yearned.
Noncents! A penny saved is no longer money, at least in Oz. We now put them into socks to make paperweights and blackjacks.

The best laid plans of mice need a translator.
Yes, Douglas Adams!

A picture is worth a million words. Ain't inflation terrible!
Correction: With trick photography and computer graphics, a picture is now only worth one's *word.*

The meek shall inherit the dirt. *But not the property rights.*

All roads lead to roads, yet no roads lead to Rhodes.
Isn't life strange?

So much to do, so little point.

Who do you think you were? reincarnationist chit-chat
Who do you think *you* were? insulted gunslinger chit-chat as he fires

13B. **SOME UNHEATED ADVICE**
(MORE NEO-TRUISMS)

If you can't stand the heat, get out of the oven. — *Forrest Gump*

If life gives you a lemon, make lemonade. But if life gives you a pickle, you might as well give up—pickleade is disgusting.
— *Clifton J. Gray*

Don't drive standing up through the sun roof while closing it.
— *car owner's manual, Dim Wit*

Never do your shoelaces up in a revolving door. — *Adeye Churchill*

Do not on any account attempt to write on both sides of the paper at once. — *W. C. Sellar and R. J. Yeatman*

Don't forget to cross your eyes and dot your teas.

Do as I *say*, not as you say.

I hate advice unless I'm giving it. — *Jack Nicholson*

Go and sell all you have, and borrow all you can, and give it to the rich. It's good for the economy.

Some people are too smart for my own good.
Beware of geeks bearing gifts.
The road to hell is paved with good inventions.

Progress is our most important problem. — *Laugh-in*

Never speak ill of the ill.

Don't put the course before the hart.
You cannot serve golf and mammals.

Don't put all your sperm in one basket.

Don't put all your monkeys in one barrel.

Never look a gift river horse in the mouth.

Don't burn your bridges before you come to them.

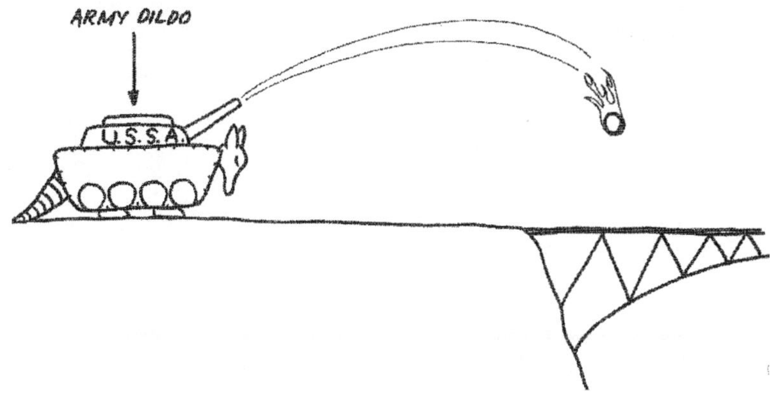

A wise man changes his mind, a miser minds his change, a fool minds any change. *Everything changes accept change!*

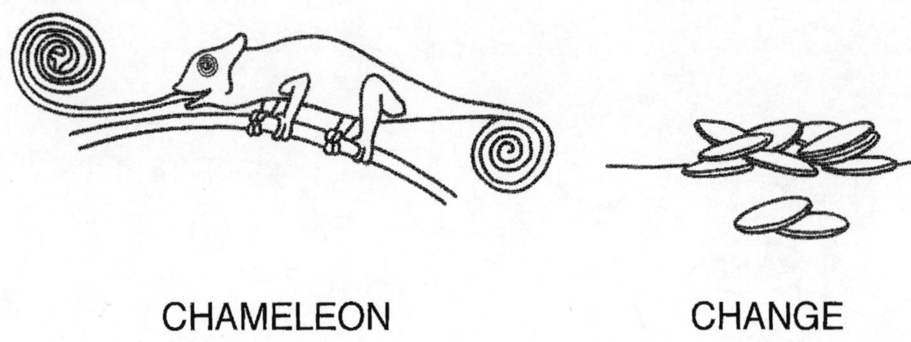

CHAMELEON CHANGE

If you're not part of the solution you haven't dissolved yet.

You have to crack an ego to make an Om.

Ask no questions, I'll tell you know lies.

When in doubt, celebrate!

Chapter 14. **SENTENCE CARRIED OUT**

Bacon wrote Shakespeare. *..regularly.* *— Anon.*

I am pushing sixty. *..that's enough exercise for me. — Mark Twain*

[boxer] ***floats like a butterfly.*** *..and stings like one too. — Brian Clough*

Many well known sayings have entered our language in a foreshortened, hence misleading form. I set the record straight by publishing the original, complete sentences. More in the August 2008 *Word Ways*.

You can't see the forest for the trees. ..have all been felled.

The whole world's a waste basket. ..case.
The old litter-and-pollute motto is brought home by disheartened antipolluters.

Blondes have more fun. ..made of them.

Clothes make the man. ..itchy-sweaty-stinky underneath.

Love makes the world go round. ..the bend.

A FOR-GONE CONCLUSION

She went for him. ..in a big way, so much so that...
She went for him. ..to the meeting—while he was out two-timing her! So...
She went for him. ..with a butcher knife.

Nice guys finish last.
..as a courtesy.

The world is my oyster.
..I have no other pets or friends.

It'll be a cold day in hell...
after the sun explodes and earth is atomised into outer space.

The customer is always right. ..tedious.

Everyone is innocent until proven guilty. ..or disliked.

Stand up for your rights. ..in a long, slow queue.

Everything fell in place. ..of rising or holding steady. (2008)

Don't trust anyone over thirty. ..seconds.

If looks could kill... it would solve the voyeur problem.

When the cat is away the mice will play.
..dice with the Universe. (*Hitchhiker's Guide to Einstein's Sayings.*)

History repeats itself. ..when Prof reuses old lecture notes.

Resist not evil, but overcome evil with good. ..bombs.
(*Neocon-cum-Tea Party Bible* 1:1, "Don't argy with 'em.")

Might makes right. ..wingers.

overthrowing the government by force -ps

All men are mortal. ..enemies, say free market darwinists.

Touch bottom. ..and get slapped in the face.

One foot in the grave...
one in the frivolous, that's my philosophy.

A word to the wise is sufficient.
..but it takes two words to dismiss a wise guy.

Politicians are not the masters of the people but servants of the people. ..that are the masters of the people.

Your country needs you. ..to shut up and play dumb.

Tell it like it is. ..true; sound sincere.

I should've known better. ..ways to hide my mistakes.

Everything is relative. ..except your relatives.

Putting yourself in another's shoes... is a case of
If the shoe fits, wear it. ..never mind whose it is.

Strike while the iron is hot.
..don't wait for the foursome in front of you.

When all else fails... you don't feel so stupid anymore.

Meantime... back at Greenwich...

The shit hit the fan. ..even though the fan idolised the shit.

There is no royal road to learning.
..which is why royals are butt ignorant.

Life begins at forty. ..is the Irish drinking motto.

An Irish queer is a fellow who prefers women to drink. — Sean O'Faolain

He's as stiff as a board. ..member.

Practice what you preach. ..before a mirror.

Just what the doctor ordered.. .another sports car.

Art is forever. ..boasting.

I don't give a shit. ..my vote.

Wishes won't wash dishes. ..not even dishy-washy wishes.

WISHY WASHY

Chapter 15.
SOME HALF-ASKED QUESTIONS

"How's your wife?" "Compared to what?" — *Anon.*

ROSE: Can I ask a dumb question?
DOROTHY: Better than anyone else I know. — *The Golden Girls*

I think if you know what you believe, it makes it a lot easier to answer questions. I can't answer your question. — *Dubya*

"Have you any concrete evidence of ghosts?"
"No, very few ghosts are made of concrete." — *Michael Bentine*

Lady: Isn't the weather dreadful?
Second lady: Yes, but it's better than nothing.† — *Anon. (overheard)*

15A. WHAT THE HOW???

Also better than nothing, I say, are the provocative questions raised by students here at **Ice Cool High School**, where I fail to teach. A sampler, with answers(?):

Is hairy palms considered VD? Yes, clap hands!

When speaking of them together shouldn't Cardinal Newman and Alfred E. Newman be called Cardinal and Alfred E. New*men*? Are they not both humen? Who on earth would want to speak of them together? Was this slipped in by *Mad Magazine* Spies? I want my Editor!

---

† Hypothetically, what's the mathematical probability of nothing at all existing, no universes anywhere? Appropriately, the answer is exactly zero.

NOTHINGNESS DOESN'T EXIST!

Yet it does exist vicariously through its name, whose existence I've just proved.

What's the difference between roast beef and pea soup?
Anyone can roast beef. — *Anon.*

How can you tell a tree from a jellyfish?

Answer: They look different.

u s u a l l y

TREE JELLYFISH

Why work your arse off when all you get *in the end* is an arse hole?

Do circumcised men suffer from foreskin envy? Not just me?

Does dirty dancing mean you must now bathe together?
Yes, unfortunately. To avoid this problem, keep it clean.

THE UGLY CONSEQUENCES OF DIRTY DANCING

Is there a law against raping leprechauns?
Not that I have any plans, mind you.

Why are ETs so evasive? Because they're illegal aliens? Do they lack earth cash to buy visas? Do alien abductees ever think to check their wallets afterwards?

Does familiarity breed contempt of court? Yes, but unlike any other crime you can't get a reduced sentence for contempt of court by pleading guilty.

Is sex just a bedroom's way of making more bedrooms?
Aye. "Won't you come in my parlour?" said the bedroom to the shy.
[Every time I reread this I read that "in" as "into". Did you fall into the same trap?]

Will she go down in History? *(Pardon this Class joke. Classy?)*

Why were there fewer middle age people in the Middle Ages?
Because dark ages.

If we didn't have calendars would our days still be numbered?
I imagine our days would be numbered even if we didn't have numbers.

Are Batman's "Truth, Justice and the American way" alternatives?
Core snot! — Ed.

Shouldn't acting members of the Free Fart Society get refunds at pay toilets?

TOILET GRAFFITI: Here I sit all broken hearted,
Paid to fart and then the Free Fart Society started!

Q. *Why do women wear perfume and make-up?*
A. *Because they're smelly and ugly.* — *Anon.*

Why is it that the winner of the Miss Universe contest always comes from Earth? — *Rich Hall*

(So far, Rich, so far! But you're right, it's rigged. A sinister conspiracy that reaches all the way to the judges and beyond. I know this to be true. When those ugly ETs try to enter the contest they get snuffed.)

Is suicide a capital offence? Only if by decapitation. (I considered decapitating myself once. *Why?* Doing it twice would have been unthinkable.)

Is giving away all your money a capital offence?
Only to a capitalist.

Do birds get their smarts by eating bookworms?

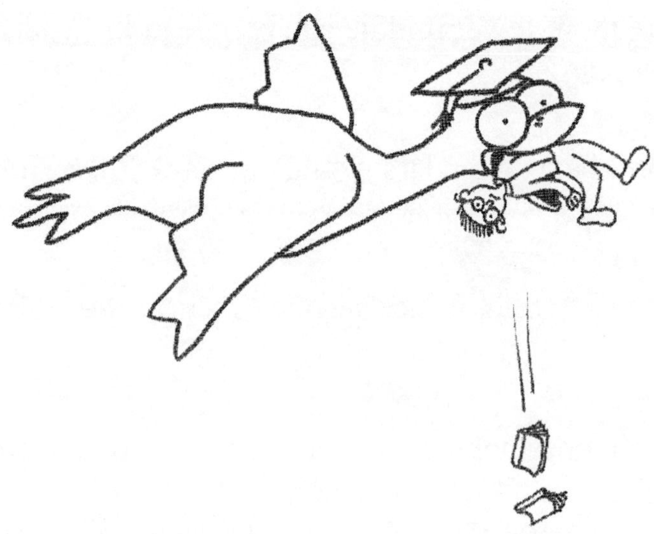

How can you tell a giraffe from a giant anteater? The giraffe is taller.

GIRAFFE GIANT ANTEATER
(eats giant ants)

Can you tell this joke from the back of a bus?
Yes, the joke is much thinner.

Which came first, the chicken or the rooster?
(Is this a dirty joke? – Ed.)
Yes, Ed, that's why she crossed the road originally.

THE CLOCK PARADOX

Why is the third hand on a clock called the second hand? And why is the big hand called the minute hand?
It all makes sense when you learn that etymologically second = minute minute.

What do you get when you cross a genius with a hooker?
A fucking know-it-all. — *Gilbert Gottfried*

What do you get if you cross The Godfather with a philosopher?
An offer you can't understand. — *Anon.*

Can you maintain a stiff upper lip with clear fingernail polish?
Is that a polish joke? Ed.

If Poles are so dumb—say those popular jokes of the '60s and '70s—why are they the only ones who can spell their names?
Yes! *Manya Sklodowska* should be a household name, but *Marie Curie* is easier.

As time seems to pass progressively faster with age, at an old enough age would time cease to exist? Is this Enlightenment?

If space is curved, as Einstein said, why aren't you smiling?
Sim, like Magellan after proving the earth is curved.

Is **artificial** a real word?

Can you find your feet by looking down on yourself?
Not if you're too far up yourself for your feet to be on the bottom. Or too fat.

Would the pharmaceutical industry promote or allege epidemics to increase its profits? Is the Pope fallible?

15B. WHY THE WHAT?? (Some Theological Riddles)

More half-asked questions, this time from unruly Sundays-cool Sunday School scholars. But first some role models I gave them.

> *I don't believe in reincarnation, and I didn't believe in it when I was a hamster.* — *Shane Richie*

> *There was an old man with a beard*
> *Who said, "I demand to be feared.*
> *Address me as God*
> *And love me, you sod."*
> *And man did just that, which was weird.* — *Roger Woddis*

> *Neither ...foolish talk, nor jesting...*
> — *Saint Paul,* instructing Christians to be humourless

> *The total absence of humor from the Bible is one of the most singular things in all literature.* — *Alfred North Whitehead*

Whitehead overlooked one of the earliest known lame puns:

> *Thou art Peter, and upon this rock I will build my church.* — *Jesus* (?)

Why is the Prince of Darkness called Lucifer, the lightbearer?

Is Islam an especially warmongering religion?

Sure. *Onward Christian Pacifists!*
Marching as to Peace!

Why are we ever so eager to pardon Jehovah for *His* heinous sins—the Flood, Sodom and Gomorrah, Pompeii, Katrina, Haiti, Thatcher, Dubya, etc?

Isn't it cheating to pray before a game? Yes, more unfair than drugs!

Why do we pester God with more G-mail on His day off than on any other? Yeah, give Him a *break!* Pray only on weekdays.

Was the Creation merely a recreation for God, something He's done infinite times before? If not, what was He doing in all that eternity BC? Why wait till now to make us?

Did **JICs** (Judeo-Islamo-Christians) celebrate October 20 1996? No. (At 9AM sharp that was the 6000th anniversary of Creation, says Bishop Ussher (1654), from adding up the begats in the Bible.) I told all I met about it at the time but couldn't arouse much enthusiasm. Missing this hexamillennial landmark shows a disrespect for the Bible bordering on blasphemy.

What is "God on High" on, anyway? Holy spirits, no doubt.
And was Jesus stoned?

Was God the original homosexual pedophile?
Yes, in a sense. He made Adam for Himself, His toy, but He made Eve for Adam, not for Himself. (Struth. Read the Bible.)

Indeed is God single? Or is a Mrs. God hidden away up there? Yes, She does all the heaven-cleaning and such while God occupies Himself with birdwatching. You know, sparrows and such.

Is it just a coincidence that, according to the numbers in the Bible, Methuselah died in the same year as Noah's flood? Was this Patriarch murdered by his own ambitious grandson by being excluded from the Ark? Or by hand *on* the Ark? Maybe it was more innocent and he died of swine flu from the squalid conditions on that cram-packed vessel that would make Philippine ferries look luxurious.

Did God really write the Bible? No, he used a Ghost writer.

Since parthenogenesis (virgin birth) can only produce females, was Jesus actually a woman in disguise? (Mary Magdalene!)

Christ died for out sins. Dare we make his martyrdom meaningless by not committing them? — *Jules Feiffer*

Would God be willing to give up His earthly possessions like He asks us to do? *That's what He's doing right now!!* Why do you think I've been studying ark building?

Chapter 15C. WHO THE WHEN?

Questionable Characters
(Name Droppings 3†)

Some Questionable Questions and Answerable Answers About the Famous

Is Tiny Tim a boy or a girl?
I don't think so. — *Alan Seus and Goldie Hawn, Laugh-In*

When I was young I always wanted to be somebody.
Now I wish I had been more specific. — *Lily Tomlin*

name-dropper

Was **Francis Assisi** for loving animals?
Of course he was for it. Who more?

Was **Karen Black** balled?
Well, she showed "balls".

Is **David Bowie** or girl?
No, silly, it's just that s/he idolises Tiny Tim.

Mel Brooks no seriousness, and doesn't **Sarah Palin** comparison?

Is **Gordon Brown** nosey? Goes without saying, he's a politician.

Was **George Washington Carver** the Mt. Rushmore sculptor?
Yes, along with his family, T. J., A. L. and T. R. Carver.

---

† Name Droppings 1&2 are chapters 6D and 7C. More in *Word Ways,* Feb '04.

Was **Alan** or **John Foster Dulles**? What an uninteresting question!

Was **Faye Dunaway** with?
This is how rumours get started! Shame shame shame. — Ed.

Did **Ezekiel** invent the spinning wheel? Howe did he do it?

Did **Jean Genet** say "Pa!"? I don't know. It's French.

Is **Billy Graham** negative?
Gram-negative bacteria. Pardon the jargon. But yes, "Hell" yes.

What did **Franz Josef Haydn** seek? the lost chord

Did **Mao Tse-Tung**?
You mean was his Little Red Book full of little brown stuff?

Is **Demi** or **Roger Moore** talented? more or less

Was **Carl Orff** that actor who played Frankenstein's monster?
Who, Boris Burana, Carmina's husband?

Was **Thomas Paine** free?
No, he p(a)ined for freedom—for everyone. Well, everyone except tyrants.

Did **Rin Tin Tin** pan alley cats? Wouldn't any self-respecting dog?

Pegasus?
If pigs could fly!

Pigs <u>can</u> fly.
Peg a suss *(<u>Sus</u> scrofa)*
hitch-hiker. That's how
SWINE FLEW.

Was **Saint Peter the Great Pumpkin Eater**?

Whoa there! You've mixed four allusions. — Ed.
Is that a record?
No, that's Peanuts.

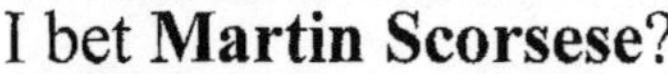

I bet **Martin Scorsese**?
I won the bet. He picked up
three girls that one night.

Did **Joseph Stalin** moral development?
Yes, one of the greatest moral runts in history.

> *Gaiety is the most outstanding feature of the Soviet Union. — Stalin*
> (Translation: outstanding = unseated, not allowed in.)

What caused **Mark Twain**? He *hasn't* waned!

Was **Oscar Wilde**? Was **Billy Wilder**?
Do bears shit in the movies?

Chapter 16. **NAME DROPPINGS 4**

Walter Mondale: *George Bush* [Sr.] *doesn't have the manhood to apologize.*
Bush: *Well, on the manhood thing, I'd put mine up against his any time.*

You can tell a lot about someone's personality by knowing his star sign: Jesus, born on December 25—fed the 5000, walked on water—typical Capricorn. — *Harry Hill*

Icarus was a soar loser. — *Anon.*

Descartes has had a few. The bartender asks if he would like another. "I think not," he says, and vanishes in a puff of logic. — *Anon.*

More pun mischief with yclept icons from **another name-dropper**.

Achilles was not well heeled.

Adam loved a good spare rib.

Charles Darwin was a misfit.
Yet he's survived, proving himself wrong!

Dracula was a neck romancer.
But ultimately a pain in the neck.

J. Edgar Hoover was a famous damn builder.

Pity poor old **Virgin Joseph**. He got no in in the womb.
No praise either. He's treated like the credulous cuckold stepfather of a bastard son. But think, if Joseph actually *did* provide the sperm for Jesus, rather than a Roman soldier named Gabriel, he was one of the greatest fathers in history.

Clark Kent never changed his underwear.

Billy the Kid wasn't wanted as a kid.

Joe McCarthy was a red hearing.

Medusa was drop-dead gorgous.

Milosevic "I'm so vile, Cosmic evil!"
These anagrams are a Serbian language quote from Milosevic's defense which by an incredible coincidence is also an unrelated English sentence. The original Serbian translates "I'm innocent of any wrongdoing. I was only giving orders."

Noah was an early entrepeneur who invested opportunely in arks.
It must've been a fleet of superarks to house the billions of animals on board, plus food for 150 days, plus feeding, sleeping, toilet, exercise and passage space.

If Noah had been very wise, He'd have swatted those two flies. — *Anon.*

Napoleon had a naughty tattoo on his hand.

Old King Cole was gay! Gay as the gay, gay month of May.
Just don't ask about those 3 "fiddlers".

Prometheus wasn't delivered by the gods, rather by eagles.
Ouch!

Shiva is a handyman. And a handy god to have around the house.

Socrates was self-seeking, hence he died of a drug overdose.

"**KING SOLOMON** IS HALVING A BABY!" town crier bulletin

Elizabeth Taylor was an ET!

Van Gogh was a ripoff artist.

Venus de Milo is a statue of limitations.

TEAM-UPS

Eartha Kitt and **Aretha Franklin** are E-motional soul sisters.

EAR^{E}THA (And anagrams. **Heart, a**?)

If **Jules Verne** collaborated with dramatist **James Shirley** (via a Medium or two) it'd be "*Le* Verne and Shirley Show".

If **Julie Ege** married **John Hammond** she would be Julie Hammond-Ege. (What a dish!)

If **Dawn French** wed **Peter Coyote** she'd be Dawn Coyote.

If **Candice Bergen** married **Charlie McCarthy** it'd be incest!
I can just hear her now, "God, what a dummy!"

And incest if **Robin Hood** wed **Little Red Riding Hood**.

If **Michael Palin** wed **Sarah Palin**, it might not be incest, but he'd be laughed out of Monty Python, she'd be a bigamist and their star-crossed kids would be freeloading Palindrones.

If **Eva Marie Saint** married **George Sanders**, he died and she married **Roger Moore**, she divorced him and wed **Yves Saint Laurent**, she'd be Eva Marie Saint Saint Saint Saint Laurent.
How much holier can you get?

THE ROYAL WATERGATE MUSIC

OR NIXON SAYS "HANDEL IT! HANDEL IT!"

Richard M. Nixon conducts the Philomoney Orchestra, with
H. R. H. "Bob" Haldeman on liar,
John Ehrlichman, synthesiser, **John Mitchell**, bagpipes,
Bebe Rebozo, loot, old-bo, **Rose Mary Woods**, fiddle, dither,
Maurice Stans, wow-wow peddle,
Unintelligible and **Expletives Deleted**, prepared tape,
Spiro Agnew, second fiddle and phonygraft,
John Wilson, winds, **Ron Ziegler**, organ,
Gordon Liddy, tamperine, **Howard Hunt**, steal getter,
Jeb Magruder, pickle-o, **Bud Krogh**, cell-o,
Melvin Laird, brass, **Alexander Haig**, military serpent,
Richard Helms, clearinit, **Henry Kissinger**, symbols,
James St. Clair, fringe horn, **James McCord**, whistle,
John Dean, repercussion [and continuo!],
Charles Colson, buffoon, **Sam Erwin**, contra-buffoon,
John Sirica, contrabase, **Daniel Ellsberg**, bare-a-tome,
Archibald Cox, surprise sacks,
Elliot Richardson, tender sacks,
the US public, rattled gourds,
David and **Julie Eisenhower**, background vocals,
Pat Nixon, accordian, and **Nixon** himself on bad vibes.

Although he was only a hemidemisemiQuaker, Nixon managed to shake up Washington with his music. Shake, rattle and (heads) roll.

Washington couldn't tell a lie, Nixon couldn't tell the truth and Reagan couldn't tell the difference. — *Mort Sahl*

Satire died the day they gave Henry Kissinger the Nobel Peace Prize. — *Tom Lehrer*

THE-OLOGY

No, this is not about *the* God, nor *the* subject or science, but *the* the word. Much grief can be wreaked, for instance, by sticking **the** into the midst of known names, eponyms and pseudo-eponyms. The altered form ideally should be redolent of the original, but some are purely comical and are not theologically correct, like Abraham the Lincoln, car man. From *Word Ways*, August, 2009.

Oedipus the Complex

Poor bloke had a "relationship" but no Freud to sort out his complexities.

J. Paul the Getty *Very* getty. And keepy.

Orville & Wilbur the Wright stuff planewrights

J. Edgar the Hoover vacuum

Old JEd cleaned up all right, infamously. But he didn't suck up to anyone. *Except his boyfriend. — Ed.*

Albert the Einstein

His name is an eponym. But some say that in fact he was no Einstein, that his name just happened to be the same as the slang term "Einstein".

W. C. the Fields. Good advice, pee and poo outdoors. For example in **George the Bush**, a protected egosystem.

Alexander the Haig Pinch

He scotched any rumours that he drank too much.

Titus the Boiled Owl Filled with the Holy Spirits?

***The* The Beatles** The the greatest! Radical beetle-beagle hybrids.

Leon the Trotsky
If Stalin was constipated, Trotsky was just the opposite.

Norbert the Wiener dog
Cybernetic dachshund from Gary Larson? Or just personifying one's wienie?

Peter the Peter pumpkin eater Beware(,) my little pumpkins!

Hershey the Bar (bar A!) Yummy.

Woody the Allen wrench A wrench is a yank-jerk.
(God wrote this, for Mia. I don't share the low opinion of love able old Woody.)

Dennis the grass-Hopper *Easy Rider* chopper hopper on grass. But no insect and no "grass" (informer, from grasshopper, rhyming slang for copper).

Mick Jagger the naughty
Fans throw themselves under him as if he were a Hindu god.

Philip the Roth of God Another naughty boy.

The the end. Not really, it's just a the end—of this chaper.

Chapter 17. **OFF COLOURFUL STORIES**

When a man fell into his ***anecdotage*** *it was a sign for him to retire from the world.* — *Benjamin Disraeli*

Sorry, Benji, I've only just started doting on anecs. But first I'll shoot myself in the foot by quoting some oldies, hoping to get laugh muscles firing unstoppably.

I was riding a horse, and its leg was broken, so I had to shoot it. Everybody on the carousel freaked out. — *Tom Cotter*

A man loses his dog, so he puts an ad in the paper that says: "Here, boy!" — *Spike Milligan*

A priest, a rabbi and a minister walk into a bar. Bartender says, "What is this, a joke?" — *Anon.*

Someone once came up to me and asked, "If you could sleep with anyone living or dead, who would it be?" And I said, "Anyone living."
— *Jimmy Carr*

ART LINKLETTER: And what do you want to do when you grow up?
KID: I want to learn the facts of life.
ART: (oh oh) And what are *the facts of life?*
KID: I don't know! — *Kids Say the Darndest Things* (radio)

MY STORY (for all three of you out there who care)

I take good care of myself, eat great heaps of diet food, brush my tooth daily, exercise my prerogatives regularly and to maintain a low carbon footprint I exhale as little as possible, especially through my feet.

MOTHER: Where'd you get that bloodstain on your crotch?
DAUGHTER: I cut myself sowing.
MOTHER: Oh, was it bad?
DAUGHTER: No, just a prick.
(PRICK: I offered her a drink and she reclined.)

YOUNG MOTHER: Doctor, doctor, my baby ate a whole bottle of Viagra! How long will he be a tripod?

YOUNG SHARK: Don't be so old-fashioned, Dad. We should evolve into one of those modern bony fish we eat all the time.

Hey, Waiter!

THE PHEASANTS
ARE REVOLTING!

THERE'S A HARE
IN MY SOUP
DON'T BLAME ME,
I'M ONLY TAKING ORDERS.

A crocodile goes into a fancy restaurant and orders "small French fries, hold the dressing." When they bring him a plate of chips, he roars "Hey, waiter! Take this back! I ordered a serve of juicy naked young garçons from the kitchen!"

"Those are the brakes," he said as she drove into a tree.

She was too short to break his heart, so she wounded his knee.
(Ta to John Hall-Freeman.)

A man is in bed with his mistress. His wife calls. He says, "Sorry, Dear, I can't make it. Something's come up."

To keep his cool this guy packs ice around it.

A pregnant woman gets an overwhelming desire for liver. Her husband rushes to the butcher but comes back with bad news. "They're out of liver, dear, you'll have to take heart."

CUT OUT LIVER, PREGNANT WOMEN TOLD — *Northern Echo* headline

The American Dream began in 1898 with cuddly old Teddy Bear Roosevelt's impassioned call to *"Charge!!"*
Abject patriotic obedience ensued, as did the later, inevitable debt crisis.

"Where can we hide?" squeaked 11 to 111 in a panic. "Quick! In here among the els." said 111. It worked beautifully!

111111111111111111111111111111111111111111111111

Now, where's Wa11111y? (This trick will work for any one.)

When the cops found cannabis in the botanist's greenhouse he screamed, "This is a *plant!*"

SOME DOOMSDAY SCENARIOS

1. Noah's ark sank. End of history.
2. Noah, not believing God, never built the ark. End of history.
3. Noah's children, not believing all the warnings, don't act in time to prevent another world-wide 'flood'. End of history.

A flying saucer lands and just sits there. A week later after a huge crowd has gathered a jolly green giant emerges and says, "You're probably wondering why I've brought you here."
(Private alien joke. Get it? I didn't either.)

"Giant ET, my foot!" said the skeptic. The giant overheard, accepted his offer, and wears it as a lucky charm. And the skeptic's gang mocks him when he tells how he lost his foot.

Vincent painted his name on his van in big letters. When he sped by he wanted folks to say "Look at that Vincent van go!"

When they built a highway right over the grave of Farmer Jones' beloved Champion rooster, he couldn't stop grieving. *"Why did the road cross the chicken?"*

A dear friend of mine used to eat a lot of pine cones. When I told him that they were poisonous, he died. This is a ~~good~~ bad example of a **self-fulfilling rumor**.
Am I confessing manslaughter? HAHA only joking! Hee-hee. Okay I did it.

You remember the militant lesbian psychopath who liberated men's penises and collected them in the back of her panel van? The Media called her the dick van dyke. I recently unearthed the fact that she called her van the peter lorry.

Once upon a time a giraffe fell in love with a cherry-picker. It was a plucky and sweet romance, but whatever did the cherry-picker see in the giraffe? Still, who am I to ridicule? I once fell in love with a broomstick mistaking it for a fashion model.

A time traveller lands in 2013 and asks a stranger *[Stranger? Is anything stranger that a time traveller?]*, "Excuse me, sir, I've come from 1913, from the Age of Invention, and I'm dying to know if there have been any new inventions or developments since."

The other day a cockroach was sitting on the rim of the toilet when I thoughtlessly intruded upon its territory and urinated. That cockroach was truly pissed off.

panish buns in **bunish pans**

Punish bans!

Br'er Warren Warden was a pathologically serious rabbit who conspired to **banish puns**. When they exposed his heinous plot he feigned ignorance and shock. When the evidence became overwhelming he feigned remorse and trepidation. "Please, do anything but don't throw me in the drier patch!" And it was this one atrocious pun that saved him from the wrath of the lighthearted mob. But remember, I'm talking rabbits here. Most of us sad humans would support the plot.

My dog is named Preamble: he's always weeing the people.

Fish out of water lose their aqueous humour. *Not funny! Ed.*

"Stick your money where the sun never shines!" I told a miser. "No problem, it's already there," he said smugly.

1) Gone are the days when our hearts were young and homo...
2) Gone are the days when our hearts were young and cheerful-but-not-gay...
revisions of the song *Old African American Joe:* 1) = Newspeak; 2) = PC

A mate told me he was in Baltimore walking along during an air-raid drill (bomb-attack practice run) when approached by the police. "*You! What're you doing out during an air raid?*" they barked. "It's okay," he replied gently, "I'm a suicide."

New Revelations is the title of a book I found in the desert, by God (or Gob or Gog? I couldn't make it out). It told of a future day when God (or Gob or Gog) in His infinite compassion repents and lets everyone into Heaven. "I was just kidding about Eternal Damnation," He says meekly. "What?" scream the True Christians as they stormp out of Heaven in protest, "We were *good for nothing*??" "No, No, come back," says God (or Gob or Gog), "there is a reward! Only you, My true loves, get to sit on My Right Hand and spend eternity praising Me!" And He casts the others, the sinners, out into the antechamber of Heaven where the poor souls were obliged to occupy themselves forever in godless (or gobless or gogless) behaviour.

Chapter 18. **PUNCH (DRUNK) LINES**

Confessions and Astray Thoughts

The business of the government is to keep the government out of business — that is, unless business needs government aid. — *Will Rogers*

A bank is a place that will lend you money if you can prove that you don't need it. — *Bob Hope*

Banking establishments are more dangerous than standing armies. — *Thomas Jefferson*

If you would know what the Lord God thinks of money, you have only to look at those to whom He gave it. — *Maurice Baring*

As a general rule, no one has money who ought to have it. — *Benjamin Disraeli*

What we have in this country [USA] *is socialism for the rich and free enterprise for the poor.* — *Gore Vidal*

I suppose if I'm absolutely honest, I use my penis as a sort of car substitute. — *Stephen Fry*

It's the blackest day for Grand Prix racing since I started covering the sport. — *Murray Walker*

I never comment on referees and I'm not going to break the habit of a lifetime for that prat. — *Ron Atkinson*

Footballers are no different from human beings. — *Graham Taylor*

We're fools whether we dance or not, so we might as well dance. — *Japanese proverb*

I watch tennis because I like to see things change directions.

I have a big collection of boomerangs I can't seem to get rid of.

I've been called a plagiarist. I think I can use that.

Damn those who have made my remarks before me!
— *Aelius Donatus* (*c.* 350 AD)

I wouldn't mind if I lost my mind. How could I?
I'd be a solipsist if it were socially acceptable.

I won't relax until I learn to *relax*.
"Peace of mind is only in your mind." my mind keeps re-minding me.

Shut up, echo!! Shut up, echo!! Shut up, echo!! Shut up, echo!!

I'm inclined to play fast and lose.

I ran high hurdles in the Nude Olympics. It's why I talk funny.

I hold nothing against porcupines, mind you.

I'll never be able to look an octopus in the face. I don't know how to find it. I only studied science so I could understand science jokes.

"*What about plastic toymaker jokes?*" you ask. I don't get it. I'm science.

I find snowflakes very sixy, if anyone cares.

SNOWFLAKES: **S**ixfold **N**odes **O**f **W**ater
Forming **L**ovely **A**nd **K**aleidoscopic '**E**phemeral **S**tones'
These 'gemstones' were a window into the atomic level of reality available 13,700,000,000 years before *H. sap* came along. Did any ancient philosophers eg Pythagoras see them in that light? Or care, as I do.

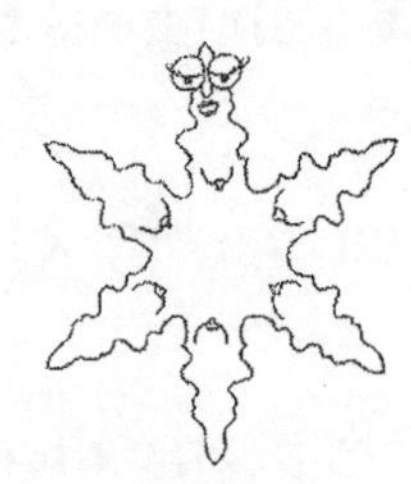

I finally got my shit together, then I forgot where I put it.
I'm so dumb I keep forgetting that I'm dumb.

He's suffering from Clue Deficit Disorder. — Anon.

Noses run in our family.
Mother the genealogist told me so.

Don't read this sentence. Too late!

One thing *I* learned too late
is that ignorance is bliss.
But if I'd known that earlier,
I would't have been ignorant.
This is catch 23.

Families, when a child is born, wish it to be intelligent. But I, through intelligence having wrecked my whole life, only hope the baby will prove ignorant and stupid. Then he will crown a tranquil life by becoming a Cabinet Minister.
— *Su DongPo* (1090)

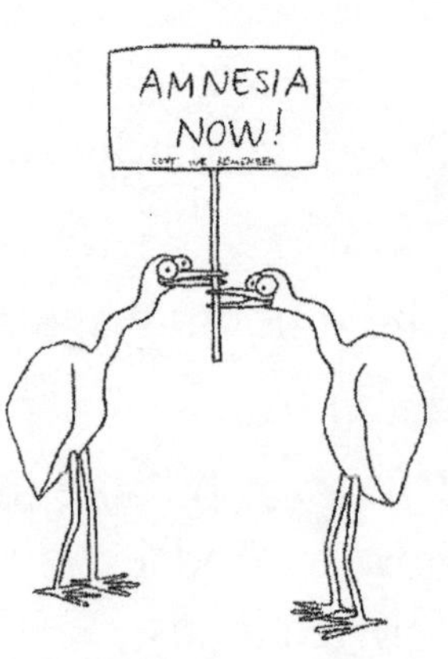

egrets' regrets

I say "Morning!"† to everyone I meet on my AM walks. It's a community service, in case anyone thinks it's PM.

† The "Good" is silent, as in

All it takes for evil to triumph is for good men to say nothing. — *Anon.*

I used to be a left-winger. Now I'm a left-over.

Yet I keep hearing voices saying, *"Save your southpaw moustache cups, gang, the Left shall rise again!"*

I want to live in the present in the future.
Not that I've never lived in the present in the past.

Every time I start a diet I soon dessert it.

Diets are for those who are thick and tired of it. — *Anon.*

I went on a diet, swore off drinking and heavy eating,
and in fourteen days I lost two weeks. — *Joe E. Lewis*

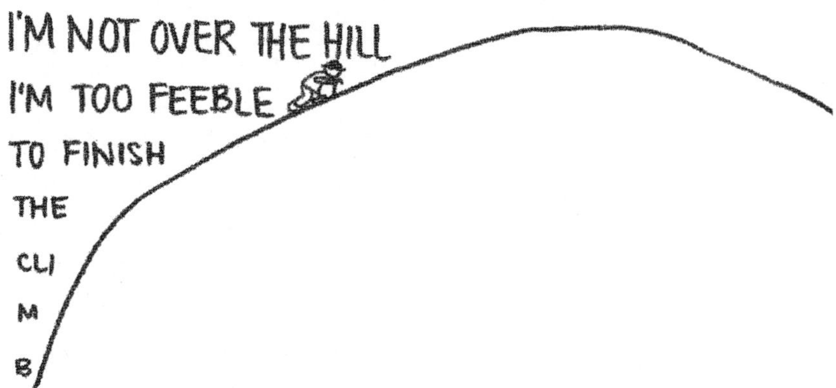

ASTRAY THOUGHTS

Nothing becomes a woman like a little girl.

Backward time travel is unbecoming.

Beauty is only skin deep, so don't skin your sweetheart.

Oh, for the good old days before butter got margarinalised.

Four-thirds of all advertising claims are exaggerations.

Perhaps our biggest mistake was when we legalised lawyers.

Pick a random number other than 19.

Did you figure out that the correct answer is nineteen?

Life is like a pinball game. If you win, your prize is you get to play on.

The DNA from one blue whale would stretch from here to Proxima Centauri.† Has NASA thought of this?

† Our nearest star, 4.2 light years away. At 9.5 trillion km per l.y. that's about 40 quadrillion metres. We and whales have about 2 metres of DNA per cell. We have 10-50 trillion cells (estimates vary) =20-100 trillion m of DNA. The whale by weight should have 2000 times as much, or 40-200 quadrillion metres. At 200 qm it could reach any of hundreds of nearby stars. Aren't whales cosmic!

Note to NASA, ESA, CSA and JSA: Send royalty cheques c/o the publisher.

Saving trees is for the birds.

Joints make you articulate. But too many joints will make you inarticulate. For example, your legs fall off.

People who say “time is money” don’t know their cash from a hole in the ground of being.

To make ends meet, fold it. Or for a 2-volume book, shelve it. Check?

> *The safest way to double your money is to fold it over and put it in your pocket.* — *Kin Hubbard*

Limbo is a hot dancehall where minor sinners are broken in to the Inferno by degrees so it’s less noticeable. Like in cookery to bring a frog slowly to the boil so it won’t notice and won’t jump out, while it will if dropped directly into boiling water. *“Who in hell eats whole boiled-live frogs?”* you ask. It’s a technique Packard’s *Hidden Persuaders* borrowed from French chefs and perfected over the years.

God made man in His own image. Doesn’t say much for God.

If the Vatican hadn’t lost hegemony over much of the world and had continued to persecute heretics, we wouldn’t have free thought, science, technology, capitalism, the industrial revolution, modern medicine, overpopulation, mass starvation or the ecological crisis they were merely trying to save us from.

Untouchables: the lowest class in India, the highest elsewhere.

If aliens are here after earth's resources, they'd better hurry.

HEALTH WARNING: Consumerism causes consumption! It's driving everyone **cravy**. If we keep consuming like there's no tomorrow, we'll be right. In the **end I**
end in
ending-
sending
spending!

We're turning the tree of life into the telephone pole of life. In a hundred years time (if there is one) Creationists will be able to claim not only that we don't come from apes but that apes never existed:

> *"It's just another atheistic scientific lie. There's no such thing as apes. Show me one! Not some old fake movies!"* — *anon*

SILLYGISMS

These hokey syllogisms proved I'm mental and helped me avoid the draft. But I didn't avoid a stern rebuke from the Man Upstairs.

1 . <u>The pen is mightier than the sword.</u>
PROOF: The pen is mightier than the thorn.
The thorn is mightier than the lion.
The lion is mightier than the swordsman.
The swordsman is mightier than the sword. QED

Even *I* could win a fight against a sword. It just lies there, like Androcles' lion. The pen can run all over one. The common, erroneous view (pictured), before I refuted it, was that the sword is mightier than the pen. What, is the sword self-actuated?

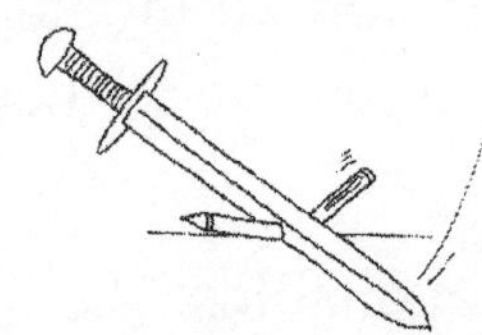

2. <u>Cunnilingus and fellatio are impossible together.</u>

PROOF: 6 may come before 9, but 9 doesn't come before 6. If they don't come before each other, they can't meet. QED.

I'm discounting simultaneous orgasm. Only $350.

3. <u>God is odd.</u>

PROOF: God is One. One is odd. QED

Or for Trinitarians, God is Three. Three is odd.

4. <u>Adam and Eve are shit.</u>

PROOF: Adam and Eve are two. "Two" is shit. QED

Boy is God gonna be pissed at you, Anil! — Ed.

5. <u>God *is* pissed!</u>

PROOF: God is One. "One" is pissed. QED

I also noted in an earlier chapter that God might be one.

6. <u>God is Swiss.</u>

PROOF: God is a Watchmaker. QED

Further proof: the God of tennis is Swiss.

7. <u>You don't exist!</u> PROOF: First an anecdote.

> SHE: Everybody loves chocolate!
> HE: I don't!
> SHE: Well, you're not everybody are you?

Since nobody is everybody, everybody is nobody. Everybody doesn't exist. This means you, you nobody. QED.

CURSES, EUPHEMISED AGAIN!

Mother taught us how a Quaker cusses you out without using obscenities:

> *I hope when thou goeth home that thy mother cometh out from under the steps and biteth thee. — Anon.*

I like Quakers (except Nixon the hemidemisemiquaker), so I thought, what the perdition, let's expand their repertoire of p.c. expletives.

I hope when thou goeth home that thy *offspring* cometh out from under the steps and biteth thee.

Methinks thy parents forgot to take the Holy vows.

Mayest thou enjoy thy dinner with thy friends the Scarabs and their cute little larvae.

It be a marvel how thou managed to *become* the very trench ye digged for thy donkey.

I pray the Lord wouldst transport thee to a warmer clime.

I urgently request that thou goeth and attendeth to thy self-abuse elsewhere. Or hie thee to some fallen soul with whom to have an unspeakable acquaintance.

Thou resembleth the gateway through which thou entered this world. And thou art well known to have re-entered that selfsame gateway.

Wouldst thou do the earth a favour and go personally water some distant patch of land. Perchance drop into that patch and even more abundantly fertilise the earth.

BIBLIOFILE V. Future Tittles 5

Einstein and His Relatives
His mother made him do it! A story as startling as Oedipus Rex.

An Anthology of North and South Polish Jokes
Real icebreakers from the ends of the earth.

Attack of the Killer Bushes
Sequel to *Day of the Triffids*, a diverting political SF thriller. Also practical for rolling cigarettes. Ironically, it's too coarse for toilet paper.

Fear of Cleavage: The Private Hell of a Cell
No relation to misogyny, or communism, this is the amoeba's story. The loss of half of its self when it cleaves in two is so traumattic it devotes the rest of its life to dreading and trying to put off the next cleavage.

Electron Microscopy of the Yin-Yang Interface
How solid is the thin divide between female and male energy? It's not. At high mag it's riddled with microwormholes and quantum tunnels connecting the two sides. They're continuous.

Aesthetic Sacrifice Rations and Quantitative Pragmatic Axiology
My theory of how beauty and ugliness should be shared equally by everyone. I'll also examine the radical sweet and sour view that they always are.

The Paper Bag as a Solution to Philosophical Problems
Make all those deep, confronting questions just go away. I'll survey the great variety of lovely fashion bags available as head coverings.

I was going to buy a copy of The Power of Positive Thinking *and then I thought: What the hell good would that do?* — *Ronnie Shakes*

Journey to the Farthest Stars in Search of Our Inner Nature
A round-about argument that each of us *is* the center of the Universe after all.

The Age of Treason: First Sedition
It started way back *Then* when Satan's agent, woman, betrayed God's firstborn and got him evicted from Paradise. I'll go on to show that every treasonous act in history was committed or caused by a woman and prove that Women's Lib is an Atheistic, Satanic, Communist, Liberal, Progressive conspiracy.

The Aging of Reason: a Study of Moderan Cultrul Senscnce
The older I get the sicker my culture seems to get. Both sick nauseated and sick nauseating. Is this real or merely the effect of greater knowledge or of age itself on my judgement? Read and decide. Send me your opinions, not.

Sanity: Its Prevention and Cure
Includes tips for the sanity-challenged on how to fake it, plus proven methods for curing the opposite, more serious Acquired Insanity Deficiency Syndrome.

Yoga, Yoghurt and You
Three Y's reasons to explore the esoteric alternative to lollygobble bliss bombs.

Meeting Yourself Halfway, or The Middle as an End in Itself
As in the Arrowbiography: ... → → → → → ↑ ← ← ← ← ← ...

The End as an End-in-Itself

QUOTATIONS INDEX (+ 60 *Anon.*, scattered)

THE **THE END.**